may '94

Locomotor Activities

by Janet A. Wessel and Ellen Curtis-Pierce

Fearon Teacher Aids

Simon & Schuster Supplementary Education Group

Designed and Illustrated by Rose C. Sheifer

ISBN-0-8224-5354-1

Printed in the United States of America

1. 9 8 7 6 5 4 3 2 1

Contents

Meeting Special Needs of Children

AIMS OF THE PROGRAM

In any class, one or more students may be unable to play and perform basic motor skills effectively. If these students can't play, run, jump, and throw at an early age, they may be slow to develop essential motor skills as well as other basic learnings and social skills—or not develop them at all.

Play is a child's way of learning and integrating skills that will be used throughout life. Through play, children come to understand the world about them. Through play, children learn to move and move to learn. And as children gain play and motor skills, their feelings of self-worth and their positive self-images grow.

Most children learn to play and move through the activities of childhood. They learn by interacting with the environment and with their brothers and sisters and their peers. Handicapped children and other children with special needs often lack the opportunities to play with their peers. These children do not develop play and motor skills on their own. They need a structured, sequential curriculum to interact with their peers, gain feelings of self-worth, and achieve success—and the sooner these children can begin such a program, the better.

This Play and Motor Skills Activities Series presents a program of effective instruction strategies through which all children can achieve success in the general physical education program. It is not a pull-out program (that is, the child is not pulled out for therapy or special tutorial assistance); it is not a fix-it program (that is, the child is not segregated until all deficits are remediated). It is a positive program for each child to succeed in a play-and-motor-skills activity program. It is designed to help you, the teacher, set up sequential curricula, plan each child's instructional program, and teach effectively so that each child progresses toward desired learning outcomes.

Three Major Aims of the Program

1. To enable each child to perform basic play and motor skills at the level of his or her abilities;

2. To help each child use these skills in play and daily living activities to maximize his or her health, growth, and development, as well as joy in movement; and

3. To enhance each child's feelings of self-worth and self-confidence as a learner while moving to learn and learning to move.

BOOKS IN THE SERIES

There are eight books in this Play and Motor Skills Activities Series for preprimary through early primary grades, ages 3–7 years.

1. Locomotor Activities
2. Ball-Handling Activities
3. Stunts and Tumbling Activities
4. Health and Fitness Activities
5. Rhythmic Activities
6. Body Management Activities
7. Play Activities
8. Planning for Teaching

The seven activities books are designed to help teachers of children with handicaps and other special-needs children. Each book provides sequential curricula by skill levels. Each book is complete within its cover: sequential skills and teaching activities, games, action words, and checklists for the class's record of progress in each skill and an Individual Record of Progress (IRP) report.

Book 8, *Planning for Teaching*, is an essential companion to each of the seven activities books because it presents not only the steps for planning a teaching unit and providing for individual differences in each lesson, but it also includes a guide to incorporating social skills into units and lessons and also outlines a Home Activities Program. These two guides are particularly important for children with special needs. Because they often have limited opportunities to interact with their peers, these children need planned, sequential learning experiences to develop socially acceptable behaviors. And because special-needs children also often need extensive practice to retain a skill and generalize its use, a Home Activities Program, planned jointly by parents and teacher, can give them the necessary additional structured learning opportunities.

SEQUENTIAL CURRICULA: SUCCESS BY LEVELS

Each child and the teacher evaluate success. Success is built into the sequential curricula by levels of skills and teaching activities.

Each skill is divided into three levels: rudimentary Skill Level 1 and more refined Skill Levels 2 and 3. Each level is stated in observable behavioral movement terms. The skill levels become performance objectives. Children enter the sequential program at their own performance levels. As they add one small success to another and gain a new skill component or move to a higher skill level, they learn to listen, follow directions, practice, create, and play with others.

Within each skill level, your activities are sequenced, so the child can gain understanding progressively. Within each skill, you provide cues to meet each child's level of understanding and ability. The continuum of teaching cues is

1. verbal cues (action words) with physical assistance or prompts throughout the movement,

2. verbal cues and demonstrations,

3. verbal challenges and problem-solving cues such as "can you?" and

4. introduction of self-initiated learning activities.

GAMES

Game activities are identified for each performance objective by skill level in the seven activity books. At the end of each activity book is an alphabetized description of the games. This list includes the name of each game, formation, directions, equipment, skills involved in playing, and the type of play. Just before the list, you'll find selection criteria and ways to adapt games to different skill levels. Many of the game activities can be used to teach several objectives.

ACTION WORDS

Words for actions (step, look, catch, kick), objects (foot, ball, hand), and concepts (slow, fast, far) are used as verbal cues in teaching. These action words should be matched to the child's level of understanding. They provide a bridge to connect skill activities with other classroom learnings. In the seven activity books, action words are identified for each performance objective by skill level, and an alphabetized list of Action Words is provided at the beginning of each book. As you use this program, add words that are used in other classroom activities and delete those that the children are not ready to understand.

CHECKLISTS:
A CHILD'S RECORD OF PROGRESS

In each activity book, you'll also find Individual and Class Records of Progress listing each performance objective. You can use one or both to record the entry performance level and progress of each child. The child's Individual Record of Progress can be used as part of the Individualized Educational Program (IEP). The teacher can record the child's entry performance level and progress on the child's IEP report form or use the end-of-the-year checklist report.

By observing each child performing the skills in class (e.g., during play, during teaching of the skill or in set-aside time), you can meet the special needs of each child. By using the checklists to record each child's entry level performance of objectives to be taught, you can develop an instructional plan for and evaluate the progress of each child.

Assign each child a learning task (skill component or skill level) based on lesson objectives, and plan lesson activities based on the entry performance level to help the child achieve success. Then use the checklists to record, evaluate, and report each child's progress to the parents. With this record of progress, you can review the teaching-learning activities and can make changes to improve them as necessary.

TEACHING STRATEGY

Direct Instruction

Direct Instruction is coaching on specific tasks at a skill level that allows each child to succeed. A structured and sequential curriculum of essential skills is the primary component of Direct Instruction. As the child progresses in learning, the teacher poses verbal challenges and problem-solving questions such as "can you?" and "show me!" Direct Instruction is based on the premise that success builds success and failure breeds failure.

Adaptive Instruction

Adaptive Instruction is modifying what is taught and how it is taught in order to respond to each child's special needs. Adaptive Instruction helps teachers become more responsive to individual needs. Teaching is based on the child's abilities, on what is to be taught in the lesson, and on what the child is to achieve at the end of instruction. Lesson plans are based on the child's entry performance level on the skills to be taught. Students are monitored during instruction, and the activities are adjusted to each student's needs. Positive reinforcement is provided, and ways to correct the performance or behavior are immediately demonstrated.

Children enter the curriculum at different skill levels, and they learn at different rates. The sequential curriculum helps teachers to individualize the instruction for each child in the class. Thus, the same skill can be taught in a class that includes Betty, who enters at Skill Level 1, and James, who enters at Skill Level 3, because the activities are prescribed for the class or group, but the lesson is planned in order to focus on each child's learning task, and each child is working to achieve his or her own learning task. What is important is that each child master the essential skills at a level of performance that matches his or her abilities, interests, and joy.

Since children learn skills at different rates, you might want to use the following time estimates to allot instructional time for a child to make meaningful progress toward the desired level of performance. One or two skill components can usually be mastered in the instructional time available.

120 minutes	180 minutes	240 minutes	360 minutes
▲	▲	▲	▲

Higher Functioning Faster Learner   Slower Functioning Slower Learner

Locomotor Skills and Activities

INTRODUCTION

Goals for Each Child

1. To demonstrate the ability to perform basic locomotor skills taught in the instructional program;

2. To use locomotor skills in daily living activities in order to maximize healthy development and joy in movement; and

3. To gain greater feelings of self-worth and self-confidence and to gain greater ability in moving to learn and learning to move.

Locomotor skills contribute to each child's ability to move effectively in school, at home, and in the community. Their primary developmental contribution is to strength, endurance, speed, balance, agility, and general body coordination. These important attributes are necessary to a child's success in all activities.

In every classroom, one or more students may be unable to perform basic locomotor skills effectively. This inability can delay or prevent the development of later sport skills as well as important cognitive and social skills.

As components of basic locomotor skills are acquired during the preschool and early elementary years, children move from an immature pattern to a refined and mature pattern as they enter elementary programs. But motor skill acquisition does not proceed at a consistent rate for any child. A child may experience a period of rapid change in motor behavior with the acquisition of new skills followed by a plateau in which little change occurs. Or a child may acquire a skill but perform it inconsistently, because it takes time to integrate the skill into play and daily activities at home and at school.

The special-needs child, although following a similar sequential order, may proceed much more slowly and show greater inconsistency in the attainment of a given skill. Sometimes the skill may be absent from the child's repertoire due to lack of opportunity to participate in activities or to a condition that hinders acquisition of the skill.

Children with special needs in preschool through early elementary years require planned, structured, and sequenced motor and play activities to develop and maintain healthy growth equal to their potentials. This book presents three levels of activities for each locomotor skill in the following order:

1. Climbing
2. Running
3. Jumping
4. Hopping
5. Galloping
6. Sliding
7. Skipping

GETTING STARTED

To begin, decide which locomotor skills you will teach. You can plan a unit or a week or a day or a year. You may decide to teach all skills in this book. Or you may select just a few. Review the checklist for each skill objective you select to teach. Become familiar with the skill components. Next, decide which action words and games you will use in teaching these skills.

Action Words

The words you use are teaching cues. Select ones your children will understand. For each of the locomotor skills, action words are listed by skill level, and an alphabetized list of words for all the skills in this book is provided below. Circle the words you will use in teaching. If the words you selected prove too difficult for your students, cross them out. Add others that are more appropriate for your children. Star those words that work well.

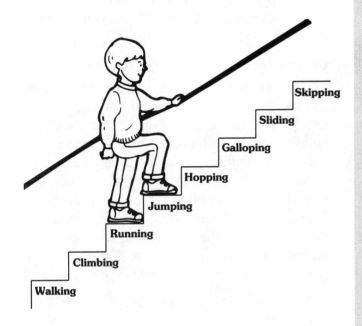

ACTION	OBJECT	CONCEPT
Bend	Arm	Around
Climb	Barrel	Behind
Crawl	Bell	Both
Gallop	Board	Do this
Go	Chair	Down
Hold	Circle	Erect
Hop	Cone	Fast
Jump	Foot	Forward
Kneel	Hand	Front
Land	Handrail	Hear
Lift	Ladder	High
Move	Lead foot	Lead
Pull	Leg	Left
Run	Line	Look
Sit	May	Near
Skip	Path	On
Slide	Railing	Other
Stand	Rear foot	Out
Step	Skip foot	Over
Step down	Stairs	Ready
Step-hop	Step	Rear
Step up	Trunk	Right
Stop	Whistle	Show me
Swing		Sideways
Turn		Through
Walk		To
		Together
		Under
		Up
		Watch

Games and Play Activities

For each skill level, you'll find a list of games; select the activity matched to the skills you plan to teach. At the end of this book, you'll find a list of games along with a description of each of them. You'll note that some of the games can be used to teach more than one skill. Use this master list to note those games and play activities that work well and those that do not. Make your comments right on the game listed, or set up a similar format for the games you have selected and make your comments on that sheet. This kind of information can help you plan successful teaching activities.

Equipment

One or more of the following pieces of equipment will be needed for most of the locomotor activities and games:

1. Whistle for signals
2. Benches or boxes of varying heights (5- to 8-inch rise)
3. Stairs without handrails (4–8 steps with 3- to 8-inch rise), placed close to the wall for support and bordered by mats for safety
4. Mats or landing pads
5. Lines, colored tapes, or ropes taped to floor to mark the floor and to space equipment safely
6. Play equipment: slides, jungle gyms, ladders
7. Drum, tambourine
8. Child-size footprints cut out and glued or painted on stairs, benches, or boxes
9. Various floor and ground surfaces (carpet, foam, sand, grass)
10. Hoops, tires, and jump ropes
11. Check school resources such as stairs, curbs, steps for potential use

Space

Locomotor activities require enough space for each child to move comfortably and safely. The size of the space depends on the equipment available for the activities and games selected and on the number of children in the class. A multipurpose room and a playground are desirable.

Health and Safety

Space and the equipment should be arranged for safety (mats for landing and falling, handrails or walls for support in climbing stairs). Children with braces, crutches, or wheelchairs may need inclines or wider bases of support or lower step-rises. Children with special visual needs may need a tour of the space and equipment before the lesson. A buddy can be assigned to be near the child when the lesson is taught. Children with special hearing needs may need to be close to the teacher or leader of the activity. The teacher should be positioned to observe all the children during the lesson activities.

Organization: Learning Centers

Learning centers are one of the best types of class organization. You can plan small group learning centers when you know each child's level of performance of the locomotor skill to be taught. Learning centers can be used to group children by levels of ability or to mix children of different levels of ability. The number of learning centers and their purpose will depend on the number of teachers and support personnel: aides, parent volunteers, older peer models.

To set up a learning center, you should consider the following:

1. Purpose	Skills to be taught and practiced
2. Levels	Levels 1, 2, and 3, or only one, determined by size of class, space, equipment, support personnel
3. Grouping	Same or mixed skill levels
4. Physical setting	Location, such as playground or multipurpose room; equipment available; existing physical boundaries, such as walls, or space to make boundaries with chairs, benches, mats, tapes
5. Activities	Type of game or instructional activity such as running on paths, jumping over lines, climbing jungle gym

LEARNING CENTERS: LOCOMOTOR AND GAMES ACTIVITIES

LEARNING CENTER 1

Location: Playground

Skill: Climbing

Activity: Climbing treehouse stairs, slide, ladders, jungle gym

Grouping: Children at same or different skill levels

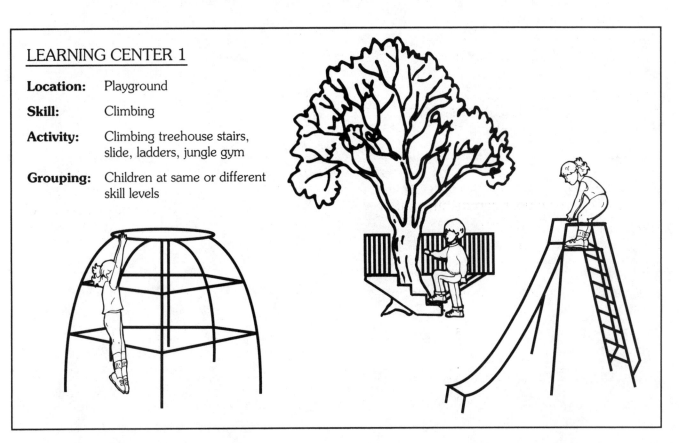

LEARNING CENTER 2

Location: Playground

Skill: Running

Activity: Running on paths, around circles, on boards

Grouping: Children at same or different skill levels

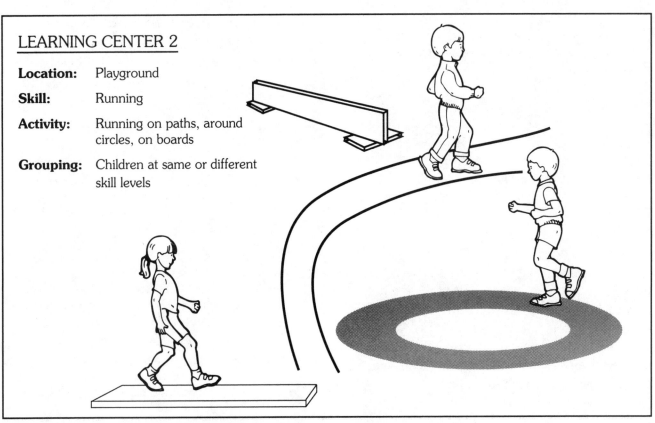

Locomotor Activities

CLIMBING UP AND DOWN STAIRS: SKILL LEVEL 1

Performance Objective

The child with ability to walk can climb up and down a flight of four to eight steps (5- to 8-inch rise), placing both feet on each step, three consecutive times, demonstrating the following skill components:

On steps with a support (handrail or other device), the child can

1. climb up (place each foot on each step before stepping on next step while holding handrail or other support for balance) and

2. climb down (place each foot on each step before stepping on next step while holding handrail or other support for balance).

Action Words

Actions: Bend, climb, go, hold, move, step, walk

Objects: Foot, hand, handrail, stairs

Concepts: Both, down, look, on, ready, show me, up

Games

- Climbing Hills, Paths
- Climbing over Snowbanks
- Climbing Races
- Climbing Ropes, Frames
- Did You Ever See a Lassie/Laddie?
- Follow the Leader
- Freeze
- Jungle Gym Tag
- Obstacle Course
- Upstairs/Downstairs

TEACHING ACTIVITIES

If a child requires assistance to respond,

1. give verbal cues and physical assistance.
Manipulate or guide the child through the entire skill. Hold the child by the hand. Take the child's leg, and place it on the first step. Take the other leg, and place it on first step. Continue process up and down stairs. Give the child specific verbal instructions throughout (in sign language, bliss symbols, action cues), such as "Climb up the stairs," "Put your foot on the first step," "Step up, go."

2. give verbal cues with demonstration.
Use a model or have the child watch you climb up and down stairs so that each foot lands on each step. Then have the child perform the action. Use specific verbal instructions (as in 1 above with the modeling).

If a child can respond without assistance,

3. give a verbal challenge in the form of a problem: "Who can . . . ?" "Show me how you can . . ."
a. Get to the top of the stairs with both feet on each step.
b. Come down the stairs with both feet on each step.
c. Variations: Use a drum and have the child move to the beat; move up and down on the footprints on the stairs; step up and down on various surfaces (soft, firm, rough, smooth, different stair heights—3–6 inches) with both feet up or down.

4. introduce self-initiated learning activities.
Set up the equipment and space for climbing. Provide time at the beginning of the lesson and free time for independent learning after the child understands the skills to be used. You may ask the child to create a game activity to play alone or with others (partner or small group) on the equipment.

5. Variations: Set up an obstacle course that includes stairs, ladders, slides, or other equipment for the child to climb up and down. Play a game, such as Follow the Leader, Freeze, Did You Ever See a Lassie/Laddie? or Upstairs/Downstairs, that incorporates climbing activities.

CLIMBING UP AND DOWN STAIRS: SKILL LEVEL 2

Performance Objective

The child with acquisition of Skill Level 1 can climb up and down a flight of four to eight steps (5- to 8-inch rise), alternating feet on each step, three consecutive times, demonstrating the following skill components:

On steps with a support (handrail or other device), the child can

3. climb up (alternate feet on each step while holding handrail or other support and maintain balance) and

4. climb down (alternate feet on each step while holding handrail or other support and maintain balance).

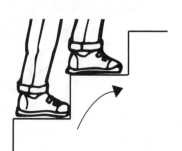 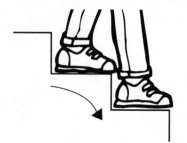

Skills to Review

1. Climb up, placing each foot on each step before stepping on next step while holding handrail or other support for balance, and

2. climb down, placing each foot on each step before stepping on next step while holding handrail or other support for balance.

Action Words

Actions: Bend, climb, go, hold, move, step, walk

Objects: Foot, hand, handrail, stairs

Concepts: Both, down, look, on, ready, show me, up

Games

- Climbing Hills, Paths
- Climbing over Snow-banks
- Climbing Races
- Climbing Ropes, Frames
- Did You Ever See a Lassie/Laddie?
- Follow the Leader
- Freeze
- Jungle Gym Tag
- Obstacle Course
- Upstairs/Downstairs

TEACHING ACTIVITIES

If a child requires assistance to respond,

1. give verbal cues and physical assistance.
Manipulate or guide the child through the entire skill. Hold the child by the hand. Take the child's leg, and place it on the first step. Take other leg, and place it on the second step. Continue this process up and down stairs. Give the child specific verbal instructions throughout (in sign language, bliss symbols, action cues), such as "Put your foot on the first step," "Put your other foot on the next step," "Step up, go."

2. give verbal cues with demonstration.
Use a model or have the child watch you climb stairs so that each foot lands on a subsequent step. Then have the child perform the action. Use specific verbal instructions (as in 1 above with the modeling).

If a child can respond without assistance,

3. give a verbal challenge in the form of a problem: "Who can . . . ?" "Show me how you can . . ."

a. Get to the top of the stairs with a different foot on each step.

b. Come down the stairs, using a different foot on each step.

c. Enter or leave school bus.

d. Enter or leave school's main office, cafeteria, bathroom, library.

e. Climb up to or down from the second story in your home.

f. Shop in the mall.

g. Climb up and down playground equipment, jungle gym, swing set.

h. Climb up and down hills, sand dunes, snow banks.

i. Variations: Use a drum and have the child move to the beat; move up and down on the footprints on the stairs; step up and down on various surfaces (soft, firm, rough, smooth), on stairs of different heights (3–6 inches).

4. introduce self-initiated learning activities. Set up the equipment and space for climbing. Provide time at the beginning of the lesson and free time for independent learning after the child understands the skills to be used. You may ask the child to create a game activity to play alone or with others (partner or small group) on the equipment.

5. Variations: Set up an obstacle course that includes stairs, ladders, slides, or other equipment for the child to climb up and down. Play a game, such as Follow the Leader, Freeze, Did you Ever See a Lassie/Laddie? or Upstairs/Downstairs, that incorporates climbing activities.

CLIMBING UP AND DOWN STAIRS: SKILL LEVEL 3

Performance Objective

The child with acquisition of Skill Level 2 or a level of performance appropriate for the child's level of functioning can maintain that level over six weeks.

Given activities that require the skill, the child can

1. play two or more games listed below at home or school, and
2. play with equipment selected by teacher and parent(s).

Skills to Review

1. Level 1: climb up, placing each foot on each step before stepping on next step while holding handrail or other support for balance, and
2. climb down, placing each foot on each step before stepping on next step while holding handrail or other support for balance.
3. Level 2: climb up, alternating feet on each step while holding handrail or other support and maintaining balance, and
4. climb down, alternating feet on each step while holding handrail or other support and maintaining balance.

Action Words

Actions: Bend, climb, go, hold, move, step, walk

Objects: Foot, hand, handrail, stairs

Concepts: Both, down, look, on, ready, show me, up

Games

- Climbing Hills, Paths
- Climbing over Snowbanks
- Climbing Races
- Climbing Ropes, Frames
- Did You Ever See a Lassie/Laddie?
- Follow the Leader
- Freeze
- Jungle Gym Tag
- Obstacle Course
- Upstairs/Downstairs

TEACHING ACTIVITIES FOR MAINTENANCE

In Teaching

1. Provide the child with teaching cues (verbal and nonverbal, such as demonstration, modeling, imitating) for climbing up and down that involve the skill components the child has achieved in compatible teaching and play activities. Bring to the child's attention the skill components he or she has already achieved. Provide positive reinforcement and feedback for the child.

2. Use games that require climbing up and down stairs and that involve imitating, modeling, and demonstrating.

3. Observe and assess each child's maintenance at the end of two weeks. Repeat at the end of four weeks (if maintained) and six weeks after initial date of attainment.

▲ Box in the skill level to be maintained on the child's Class Record of Progress. Note the date the child attained target level of performance (defined by teacher alone or co-planned with parents).

▲ Two weeks after attainment, observe the child. Is the level maintained? If child does not demonstrate the skill components at the desired level of performance, indicate the skill components that need reteaching or reinforcing in the comments sheet on the Class Record of Progress. Reschedule teaching time, and co-plan with parents the home activities necessary to reinforce child's achievement of the skill components and maintenance of attainment.

▲ Continue to observe the child, and reteach and reinforce until the child maintains that level of performance for six weeks.

▲ Plan teaching activities incorporating these components so that the child can continually use and reinforce them and can acquire new ones over the year.

▲ When the child can understand it, make a checklist poster illustrating the child's achievements. Bring the child's attention to these skill components in various compatible play and game activities throughout the year. Have the child help others—a partner or a small group.

In Co-Planning with Parent(s)

1. Encourage the parent(s) to reinforce the child's achievement of the skill components in everyday play and living activities in the home.

▲ Provide key action words for the parent(s) to emphasize.

▲ Give the parent(s) a list of play and games to use in playing with the child, thus reinforcing the skill components the child has achieved and needs support to maintain.

▲ Give the parent(s) a list of climbing activities that can be done at home with the child, such as

   a. Entering and leaving school bus.

   b. Entering and leaving school's main office, cafeteria, bathroom, library.

   c. Climbing up to and down from the second story at home.

   d. Shopping in the mall.

   e. Climbing up and down playground equipment, jungle gym, swing set.

   f. Climbing up and down hills, sand dunes, snowbanks.

2. Set up a time every two weeks to interact with the parent(s) and exchange feedback on the child's progress.

Performance Objective

The child with ability to walk can walk-run a distance of 30 feet three consecutive times, demonstrating the following skill components:

Within a clear space of 30 feet, the child can walk-run

1. for three or more periods of nonsupport (both feet alternately off the ground), with
2. arms raised in opposition to legs, elbows bent, and
3. foot placed near or on a line.

Action Words

Actions: Bend, go, run, stop, turn, walk

Objects: Arm, circle, foot, leg, path

Concepts: Around, between, fast, forward, look, on, ready, show me

Games

- Base Running
- Catching Fish
- Drop the Flag
- Duck Duck Goose
- Fish Net
- Giants and Dragons
- Hill Dill
- Hot Rods
- Jet Pilots
- Poison
- Rig-a-Jig-Jig
- Rolling Down the Tube
- Train Station

TEACHING ACTIVITIES

If a child requires assistance to respond,

1. give verbal cues and physical assistance. Manipulate or guide the child through the entire skill. Hold on to the child's hands, and walk backward, pulling the student toward you. Increase the pace until the child runs two or three steps. Repeat. Give the child specific verbal instructions throughout (in sign language, bliss symbols, action cues), such as "Run toward me," "Run fast," "Ready, go."

2. give verbal cues with demonstration. Use a model or have the child watch you run along a 24-inch-wide path. Then have the child perform the action. Use specific verbal instructions (as in 1 above with the modeling).

If a child can respond without assistance,

3. give a verbal challenge in the form of a problem: "Who can . . . ?" "Show me how you can . . ."
a. Walk-run from the starting line to touch balloons (at child's chest height).
b. Walk-run to each station and perform activity.
c. Walk-run to wall, staying between two taped lines.
d. Variations: Walk-run to beat of music, varying walking tempo and running tempo.

4. introduce self-initiated learning activities. Set up the equipment and space for running. Provide time at the beginning of the lesson and free time for independent learning after the child understands the skills to be used. You may ask the child to create a game activity to play alone or with others (partner or small group) on or around the equipment (carpet squares, taped lines, etc.).

5. Variations: Set up an obstacle course that includes colored tape, obstacles (slide, jump box, or ladder) to run around. Play a game, such as Train Station, Giants and Dragons, or Drop the Flag, that incorporates running activities.

Performance Objective

The child with acquisition of Skill Level 1 can walk-run a distance of 30 feet three consecutive times, demonstrating the following skill components:

Within a clear space of 30 feet, the child can walk-run

4. for five or more periods of nonsupport (both feet off ground), with

5. heel-toe placement (moderate speed), not flatfooted, and

6. swing leg, bent about 90 degrees.

Skills to Review

1. Walk-run for three or more periods of nonsupport (both feet alternately off ground), with

2. arms in opposition to leg action, elbows bent, and

3. foot placed near or on a line.

Action Words

Actions: Bend, go, run, stop, turn, walk

Objects: Arm, circle, foot, leg, path

Concepts: Around, between, fast, forward, look, on, ready, show me

Games

- Base Running
- Catching Fish
- Drop the Flag
- Duck Duck Goose
- Fish Net
- Giants and Dragons
- Hill Dill
- Hot Rods
- Jet Pilots
- Poison
- Rig-a-Jig-Jig
- Rolling Down the Tube
- Train Station

TEACHING ACTIVITIES

If a child requires assistance to respond,

1. give verbal cues and physical assistance.
Manipulate or guide the child through the entire skill. Hold on to child's hands, and walk backward on a path and around a circle, pulling the child toward you. Increase the pace until the child runs 30 feet. Repeat three times. Give the child specific verbal instructions throughout (in sign language, bliss symbols, action cues), such as "Run toward me," "Run fast," "Ready, go."

2. give verbal cues with demonstration.
Use a model or have the child watch you run along a 24-inch-wide path and around a circle (10-inch diameter). Then have the child perform the action. Use specific verbal instructions (as in 1 above with the modeling).

If a child can respond without assistance,

3. give a verbal challenge in the form of a problem: "Who can . . . ?" "Show me how you can . . ."

a. Run through the colored tape courses (straight line, curved line, zigzag line).

b. Run through these paths (short and long), beginning with the shorter one first.

c. Run to the line, put your beanbag in the box, and run to the finish line.

d. Run around the taped circle on the floor.

e. Variation: Use a drum and have the child run around circle to beat.

4. introduce self-initiated learning activities.
Set up equipment and space for running. Provide
time at the beginning of the lesson and free time
for independent learning after the child understands the skills to be used. You may ask the child
to create a game activity to play alone or with
others (partner or small group) on or around the
equipment (carpet squares, taped lines, etc.).

5. Variations: Set up an obstacle course that
includes colored tape, obstacles (slide, jump box, or
ladder) to run around. Play a game, such as Train
Station, Giants and Dragons, or Drop the Flag,
that incorporates running activities.

Performance Objective

The child with acquisition of Skill Level 2 or a level of performance appropriate for the child's level of functioning can maintain that level over six weeks.

Given activities that require the skill, the child can

1. play two or more games listed below at home or school, and
2. play with equipment selected by teacher and parent(s).

Skills to Review

1. Walk-run for three or more periods of nonsupport (both feet alternately off ground), with
2. arms in opposition to leg action, elbows bent, and
3. foot placed near or on a line.
4. Walk-run for five or more periods of nonsupport (both feet off ground), with
5. heel-toe placement (moderate speed), not flat-footed, and
6. swing leg, bent at 90 degrees.

Action Words

Actions: Bend, go, run, stop, turn, walk

Objects: Arm, circle, foot, leg, path

Concepts: Around, between, fast, forward, look, on, ready, show me

Games

- Base Running
- Catching Fish
- Drop the Flag
- Duck Duck Goose
- Fish Net
- Giants and Dragons
- Hill Dill
- Hot Rods
- Jet Pilots
- Poison
- Rig-a-Jig-Jig
- Rolling Down the Tube
- Train Station

TEACHING ACTIVITIES FOR MAINTENANCE

In Teaching

1. Provide the child with teaching cues (verbal and nonverbal, such as demonstration, modeling, imitating) for running that involve the skill components the child has achieved in compatible teaching and play activities. Bring to the child's attention the skill components he or she has already achieved. Provide positive reinforcement and feedback for the child.

2. Use games that require running and that involve imitating, modeling, and demonstrating.

3. Observe and assess each child's maintenance at the end of two weeks. Repeat at the end of four weeks (if maintained) and six weeks after initial date of attainment.

▲ Box in the skill level to be maintained on the child's Class Record of Progress. Note the date the child attained target level of performance (defined by teacher alone or co-planned with parents).

▲ Two weeks after attainment, observe the child. Is the level maintained? If child does not demonstrate the skill components at the desired level of performance, indicate the skill components that need reteaching or reinforcing in the comments sheet on the Class Record of Progress. Reschedule teaching time, and co-plan with parents the home activities necessary to reinforce child's achievement of the skill components and maintenance of attainment.

▲ Continue to observe the child, and reteach and reinforce until the child maintains that level of performance for six weeks.

▲ Plan teaching activities incorporating these components so that the child can continually use and reinforce them and can acquire new ones over the year.

▲ When the child can understand it, make a check-list poster illustrating the child's achievements. Bring the child's attention to these skill components in various compatible play and game activities throughout the year. Have the child help others—a partner or a small group.

In Co-Planning with Parent(s)

1. Encourage the parent(s) to reinforce the child's achievement of the skill components in everyday play and living activities in the home.

▲ Provide key action words for the parent(s) to emphasize.

▲ Give the parent(s) a list of play and games to use in playing with the child, thus reinforcing the skill components the child has achieved and needs support to maintain.

▲ Give the parent(s) a list of running activities that can be done at home with the child, such as
   a. Running together.
   b. Running after your dog.
   c. Running to the end of the playground during recess.
   d. Running on the taped circles or squares on the playground.
   e. Running to a neighbor's house down the street.
   f. Running and pushing the merry-go-round at the park.
   g. Running around the track at the school near home.

2. Set up a time every two weeks to interact with the parent(s) and exchange feedback on the child's progress.

JUMPING: SKILL LEVEL 1

Performance Objective

The child with ability to walk can jump, taking off and landing on both feet without falling, three consecutive times, demonstrating the following skill components:

Within a clear space of 10 feet, the child can jump forward one quarter of the vertical height attained by

1. preparing to jump forward, knees bent, arms extended behind body, and
2. taking off and landing on both feet, while
3. swinging arms forward with thrust of legs.

Action Words

Actions: Bend, jump, land, stand, swing

Objects: Arm, feet, legs

Concepts: Down, forward, look, out, over, ready, show me, up

Games

- Animal Tracks
- Crossing the Lake
- Follow the Leader
- Jump In and Out of Tires
- Jump, Rabbit, Jump
- Jump the Shot
- Jumping Rope
- Obstacle Course
- Pop Goes the Weasel
- Popcorn
- Stop and Go
- Toss-Jump-Pick

TEACHING ACTIVITIES

If a child requires assistance to respond,

1. give verbal cues and physical assistance.
Manipulate or guide the child through the entire skill. Stand in front of the child, and hold the child's hands. Tell the child to bend the knees and jump. As the child jumps, pull the child forward so that the child lands on the opposite side of a line. Give the child specific verbal instructions throughout (in sign language, bliss symbols, action cues), such as "Ready, set, go."

2. give verbal cues with demonstration.
Use a model or have the child watch you jump over the line, while bending your knees and swinging your arms. Then have the child perform the action. Use specific verbal instructions (as in 1 above with the modeling).

If a child can respond without assistance,

3. give a verbal challenge in the form of a problem: "Who can . . . ?" "Show me how you can . . ."
a. Jump over the rope on the ground.
b. Jump forward and land on a paper "bug" on the floor.
c. Jump over a balloon.
d. Jump on the cue "pop" while singing "Pop Goes the Weasel."
e. Variations: Use a drum and have child jump when drum beats; jump while popcorn "pops." Jump forward and land on a number of surfaces (carpeting, grass, pavement, sand).

4. introduce self-initiated learning activities.
Set up the equipment and space for jumping. Provide time at the beginning of the lesson and free time for independent learning after the child understands the skills to be used. You may ask the child to create a game activity to play alone or with others (partner or small group) on the equipment.

5. Variations: Set up an obstacle course that includes foam shapes and other play equipment. Play a game, such as Jump In and Out of Tires or Toss-Jump-Pick, that incorporates jumping activities.

JUMPING: SKILL LEVEL 2

Performance Objective

The child with acquisition of Skill Level 1 can jump, taking off and landing on both feet without falling, three consecutive times, demonstrating the following skill components:

Within a clear space of 10 feet, the child can jump forward half as far as vertical height attained by

4. taking off at about 45 degrees, with

5. knees bent, trunk flexed to absorb shock, and

6. bringing arms downward on landing, maintaining balance.

Skills to Review

1. Prepare to jump forward, knees bent, arms extended behind body, and

2. take off and land on both feet, while

3. arms swing forward with thrust of legs.

Action Words

Actions: Bend, jump, land, stand, swing

Objects: Arm, feet, legs

Concepts: Down, forward, look, out, over, ready, show me, up

Games

- Animal Tracks
- Crossing the Lake
- Follow the Leader
- Jump In and Out of Tires
- Jump, Rabbit, Jump
- Jump the Shot
- Jumping Rope
- Obstacle Course
- Pop Goes the Weasel
- Popcorn
- Stop and Go
- Toss-Jump-Pick

TEACHING ACTIVITIES

If a child requires assistance to respond,

1. give verbal cues and physical assistance. Manipulate or guide the child through the entire skill. Stand in front of the child, and hold the child's hands. Tell the child to bend the knees and jump. As the child jumps, pull the child forward so that the child lands on the opposite side of a line. Give the child specific verbal instructions throughout (in sign language, bliss symbols, action cues), such as "Jump over the line," "Ready, set, go."

2. give verbal cues with demonstration. Use a model or have the child watch you jump over the line, while bending your knees and swinging your arms. Then have the child perform the action. Use specific verbal instructions (as in 1 above with the modeling), only add "Swing your arms, too."

If a child can respond without assistance,

3. give a verbal challenge in the form of a problem: "Who can . . . ?" "Show me how you can . . ."

a. Jump over the "lake" (gap) between two mats.

b. Jump into a hula hoop or onto a carpet square.

c. Jump onto the flat paper "rocks" in the "pond" like a frog.

d. Jump like a rabbit, frog, cricket.

e. Variation: Use a drum and have child jump to beat.

4. introduce self-initiated learning activities. Set up the equipment and space for jumping. Provide time at the beginning of the lesson and free time for independent learning after the child understands the skills to be used. You may ask the child to create a game activity to play alone or with others (partner or small group) on the equipment.

5. Variations: Set up an obstacle course that includes foam shapes and other play equipment. Play a game, such as Jump In and Out of Tires, Toss-Jump-Pick, that incorporates jumping activities.

JUMPING: SKILL LEVEL 3

Performance Objective

The child with acquisition of Skill Level 2 or a level of performance appropriate for the child's level of functioning can maintain that level over six weeks.

Given activities that require the skill, the child can

1. play two or more games listed below at home or school, and
2. play with equipment selected by teacher and parent(s).

Skills to Review

1. Level 1 jump. Prepare to jump forward, knees bent, arms extended behind body, and
2. take off and land on both feet, and
3. swing arms forward with thrust of legs.
4. Level 2 jump. Take off at 45 degrees, with
5. knees bent, trunk flexed to absorb shock, and
6. bring arms downward on landing, maintaining balance.

Action Words

Actions: Bend, jump, land, stand, swing

Objects: Arm, feet, legs

Concepts: Down, forward, look, out, over, ready, show me, up

Games

- Animal Tracks
- Crossing the Lake
- Follow the Leader
- Jump In and Out of Tires
- Jump, Rabbit, Jump
- Jump the Shot
- Jumping Rope
- Obstacle Course
- Pop Goes the Weasel
- Popcorn
- Stop and Go
- Toss-Jump-Pick

TEACHING ACTIVITIES FOR MAINTENANCE

In Teaching

1. Provide the child with teaching cues (verbal and nonverbal, such as demonstration, modeling, imitating) for jumping that involve the skill components the child has achieved in compatible teaching and play activities. Bring to the child's attention the skill components he or she has already achieved. Provide positive reinforcement and feedback for the child.

2. Use games that require jumping and that involve imitating, modeling, and demonstrating.

3. Observe and assess each child's maintenance at the end of two weeks. Repeat at the end of four weeks (if maintained) and six weeks after initial date of attainment.

▲ Box in the skill level to be maintained on the child's Class Record of Progress. Note the date the child attained target level of performance (defined by teacher alone or co-planned with parents).

▲ Two weeks after attainment, observe the child. Is the level maintained? If child does not demonstrate the skill components at the desired level of performance, indicate the skill components that need reteaching or reinforcing in the comments sheet on the Class Record of Progress. Reschedule teaching time, and co-plan with parents the home activities necessary to reinforce child's achievement of the skill components and maintenance of attainment.

▲ Continue to observe the child, and reteach and reinforce until the child maintains that level of performance for six weeks.

▲ Plan teaching activities incorporating these components so that the child can continually use and reinforce them and can acquire new ones over the year.

▲ When the child can understand it, make a checklist poster illustrating the child's achievements. Bring the child's attention to these skill components in various compatible play and game activities throughout the year. Have the child help others—a partner or a small group.

In Co-Planning with Parent(s)

1. Encourage the parent(s) to reinforce the child's achievement of the skill components in everyday play and living activities in the home.

▲ Provide key action words for the parent(s) to emphasize.

▲ Give the parent(s) a list of play and games to use in playing with the child, thus reinforcing the skill components the child has achieved and needs support to maintain.

▲ Give the parent(s) a list of running and jumping activities that can be done at home with the child, such as

   a. Running and jumping into a pile of leaves.

   b. Running across the mat and jumping into the hoop, over the rope.

   c. Running and jumping over foam shapes placed around the room.

   d. Running and jumping on cue in Pop Goes the Weasel, Jack Be Nimble.

   e. Running and jumping over cracks in sidewalk.

   f. Running and jumping over puddles of water.

   g. Running and jumping over streams in the park.

   h. Jumping like a rabbit, cricket, frog.

2. Set up a time every two weeks to interact with the parent(s) and exchange feedback on the child's progress.

HOPPING: SKILL LEVEL 1

Performance Objective

The child with ability to walk can hop on one foot three consecutive times, demonstrating the following skill components:

Within a clear space of 10 feet, the child can

1. move forward, pushing off on either foot, land on the same foot, and with

2. weight balanced over support foot, maintain balance, and then

3. hop three times on one foot and three times on the other foot.

Action Words

Actions: Bend, hold, hop, lift, stand, stop, swing

Objects: Arm, foot, hand, leg

Concepts: Down, look, on, ready, show me, up

Games

- Bunny Hop
- Hoop, Hop, Jump
- Hop the Shot
- Hopping Relay
- Hopscotch
- Hot Rods
- Indian Walk Through the Woods
- Jet Pilots
- On and Off the Blanket
- Thousand-Legged Worm
- Toss-Jump-Pick

TEACHING ACTIVITIES

If a child requires assistance to respond,

1. give verbal cues and physical assistance.
Manipulate or guide the child through the entire skill. Have child stand on one foot. Hold on to child's arm (on same side as support leg). Bend the child's knee, and lift the foot to initiate the hop. Repeat for opposite foot. Give the child specific verbal instructions throughout (in sign language, bliss symbols, action cues), such as "Stand on one foot, bend your knee," "Swing your arms up and hop up," "Ready, go."

2. give verbal cues with demonstration.
Use a model or have the child watch you hop forward 10 feet. Then have the child perform the action. Use specific verbal instructions (as in 1 above with the modeling).

If a child can respond without assistance,

3. give a verbal challenge in the form of a problem: "Who can . . . ?" "Show me how you can . . ."

a. Hop on the two left (or two right) footprints to me.

b. Hop on the line to the bench.

c. Hop with a partner in place as long as you can.

d. Variation: Hop to beat of drum.

4. introduce self-initiated learning activities.
Set up the equipment and space for hopping. Provide time at the beginning of the lesson and free time for independent learning after the child understands the skills to be used. You may ask the child to create a game activity to play alone or with others (partner or small group) on the equipment.

5. Variations: Set up an obstacle course that includes hoops, tires, or ropes to hop into and over. Play a game, such as Bunny Hop, On and Off the Blanket, or Hoop, Hop, Jump, that incorporates hopping activities.

HOPPING: SKILL LEVEL 2

Performance Objective

The child with acquisition of Skill Level 1 can hop on one foot, then the other, three consecutive times, demonstrating the following skill components:

Within a clear space of 10 feet, the child can

4. with nonsupport leg bent, foot carried near midline of body, nonsupport foot near floor (6 inches), and

5. arms bent at elbows in front of body, use forward arm swing (lift) with hop to increase force, and then

6. hop five times on one foot and five times on the other foot.

Skills to Review

1. Move forward, pushing off on either foot, land on foot, and with

2. weight balanced over support foot, maintain balance, and then

3. hop three times on one foot and three times on other foot.

Action Words

Actions: Bend, hold, hop, lift, stand, stop, swing

Objects: Arm, foot, hand, leg

Concepts: Down, look, on, ready, show me, up

Games

- Bunny Hop
- Hoop, Hop, Jump
- Hop the Shot
- Hopping Relay
- Hopscotch
- Hot Rods
- Indian Walk Through the Woods
- Jet Pilots
- On and Off the Blanket
- Thousand-Legged Worm
- Toss-Jump-Pick

TEACHING ACTIVITIES

If a child requires assistance to respond,

1. give verbal cues and physical assistance. Manipulate or guide the child through the entire skill. Have child stand on one foot. Hold on to child's arm (on same side as support leg). Bend the child's knee and lift the foot to initiate the hop. Repeat for opposite foot. Give the child specific verbal instructions throughout (in sign language, bliss symbols, action cues), such as "Stand on one foot, bend your knee," "Swing your arms up and hop five times on one foot, then five times on the other foot," "Ready, go."

2. give verbal cues with demonstration. Use a model or have the child watch you hop forward five times on one foot. Then have the child perform the action. Use specific verbal instructions (as in 1 above with the modeling).

If a child can respond without assistance,

3. give a verbal challenge in the form of a problem: "Who can . . . ?" "Show me how you can . . ."

a. Hop on the five left and five right footprints on the floor.

b. Hop with a hanky in your hand and drop the hanky in the bucket.

c. Hop into the hoop, turn around, and hop back.

d. Variation: Hop to beat of drum.

4. introduce self-initiated learning activities.
Set up the equipment and space for hopping.
Provide time at the beginning of the lesson and
free time for independent learning after the child
understands the skills to be used. You may ask the
child to create a game activity to play alone or with
others (partner or small group) on the equipment.

5. Variations: Set up an obstacle course that
includes hoops, tires, or ropes to hop into and
over. Play a game, such as Bunny Hop, On and
Off the Blanket, or Hoop Hop, Jump, that incorporates hopping activities.

HOPPING: SKILL LEVEL 3

Performance Objective

The child with acquisition of Skill Level 2 or a level of performance appropriate for the child's level of functioning can maintain that level over six weeks.

Given activities that require the skill, the child can

1. play two or more games listed below at home or school, and
2. play with equipment selected by teacher and parent(s).

Skills to Review

1. Level 1 hop. Move forward, pushing off on either foot, land on same foot, and with
2. weight balanced over support foot, maintain balance, and then
3. hop three times on one foot and three times on other foot.
4. Level 2 hop. Nonsupport leg is bent, foot carried near midline of body, nonsupport foot near floor (6 inches), and
5. arms bent at elbows in front of body, use forward arm swing with hop to increase force, and then
6. hop five times on one foot and five times on the other foot.

Action Words

Actions: Bend, hold, hop, lift, stand, stop, swing

Objects: Arm, foot, hand, leg

Concepts: Down, look, on, ready, show me, up

Games

- Bunny Hop
- Hoop, Hop, Jump
- Hop the Shot
- Hopping Relay
- Hopscotch
- Hot Rods
- Indian Walk Through the Woods
- Jet Pilots
- On and Off the Blanket
- Thousand-Legged Worm
- Toss-Jump-Pick

TEACHING ACTIVITIES FOR MAINTENANCE

In Teaching

1. Provide the child with teaching cues (verbal and nonverbal, such as demonstration, modeling, imitating) for hopping that involve the skill components the child has achieved in compatible teaching and play activities. Bring to the child's attention the skill components he or she has already achieved. Provide positive reinforcement and feedback for the child.
2. Use games that require hopping and that involve imitating, modeling, and demonstrating.
3. Observe and assess each child's maintenance at the end of two weeks. Repeat at the end of four weeks (if maintained) and six weeks after initial date of attainment.

▲ Box in the skill level to be maintained on the child's Class Record of Progress. Note the date the child attained target level of performance (defined by teacher alone or co-planned with parents).

▲ Two weeks after attainment, observe the child. Is the level maintained? If child does not demonstrate the skill components at the desired level of performance, indicate the skill components that need reteaching or reinforcing in the comments sheet on the Class Record of Progress. Reschedule teaching time, and co-plan with parents the home activities necessary to reinforce child's achievement of the skill components and maintenance of attainment.

▲ Continue to observe the child, and reteach and reinforce until the child maintains that level of performance for six weeks.

▲ Plan teaching activities incorporating these components so that the child can continually use and reinforce them and can acquire new ones over the year.

▲ When the child can understand it, make a checklist poster illustrating the child's achievements. Bring the child's attention to these skill components in various compatible play and game activities throughout the year. Have the child help others—a partner or a small group.

In Co-Planning with Parent(s)

1. Encourage the parent(s) to reinforce the child's achievement of the skill components in everyday play and living activities in the home.

▲ Provide key action words for the parent(s) to emphasize.

▲ Give the parent(s) a list of play and games to use in playing with the child, thus reinforcing the skill components the child has achieved and needs support to maintain.

▲ Give the parent(s) a list of hopping activities that can be done at home with the child, such as

a. Hopping over cracks in sidewalk.

b. Hopping over moving ropes wiggled on the ground.

c. Hopping on school playground shapes painted on ground.

d. Hopping on hopscotch grid.

e. Hopping to the tree, picking up the rock, hopping back.

2. Set up a time every two weeks to interact with the parent(s) and exchange feedback on the child's progress.

GALLOPING: SKILL LEVEL 1

Performance Objective

The child with ability to walk can gallop a distance of 30 feet three consecutive times, demonstrating the following skill components:

Within a clear space of 30 feet, the child can

1. step forward with lead foot followed by step with rear foot to heel of lead foot, and during

2. a brief period of nonsupport as rear foot approaches lead foot, shift weight forward, and then

3. gallop three or more times.

Action Words

Actions: Gallop, step

Objects: Arm, foot, lead foot, leg, rear foot

Concepts: Behind, do this, forward, front, look, ready, rear, show me, together, up

Games

- Did You Ever See a Lassie/Laddie?
- Follow the Leader
- Freeze
- Gallop Tag
- Hill Dill
- Obstacle Course
- Train Station

TEACHING ACTIVITIES

If a child requires assistance to respond,

1. give verbal cues and physical assistance.
Manipulate or guide the child through the entire skill. Hold on to the child's hands. Have child take a step forward or place the foot forward. Tell the child to bring the rear foot up to forward foot or to pick it up and move it near heel of lead foot; repeat sequence. Give the child specific verbal instructions throughout (in sign language, bliss symbols, action cues), such as "Put one foot forward," "Bring your other foot up," "Step-step together-step."

2. give verbal cues with demonstration.
Use a model or have the child watch you gallop forward. Then have the child perform the action. Use specific verbal instructions (as in 1 above with the modeling).

If a child can respond without assistance,

3. give a verbal challenge in the form of a problem: "Who can . . . ?" "Show me how you can . . ."
a. Gallop across the room like a cowboy on a horse.
b. Gallop to the chair, touch the chair, and gallop back to me.
c. Gallop around the circle.
d. Variation: Gallop to the beat of the drum.

4. introduce self-initiated learning activities.
Set up the equipment and space for galloping. Provide time at the beginning of the lesson and free time for independent learning after the child understands the skills to be used. You may ask the child to create a game activity to play alone or with others (partner or small group) on or around the equipment.

5. Variations: Set up an obstacle course that includes galloping activities. Play a game, such as Cowboys and Indians, Gallop Tag, or Follow the Leader, that incorporates galloping activities.

Performance Objective

The child with acquisition of Skill Level 1 can gallop a distance of 30 feet five consecutive times, demonstrating the following skill components:

Within a clear space of 30 feet, the child can

4. with arms bent at sides, lift arms while transferring weight to forward foot and

5. lead with right foot or with left foot, and then

6. gallop five or more times.

close

step

Skills to Review

1. Step forward with lead foot followed by step with rear foot to heel of lead foot, and during

2. a brief period of nonsupport as rear foot approaches lead foot, shift weight forward, and then

3. gallop three or more times.

Action Words

Actions: Gallop, step

Objects: Arm, foot, lead foot, leg, rear foot

Concepts: Behind, do this, forward, front, look, ready, rear, show me, together, up

Games

- Did You Ever See a Lassie/Laddie?
- Follow the Leader
- Freeze
- Gallop Tag
- Hill Dill
- Obstacle Course
- Train Station

TEACHING ACTIVITIES

If a child requires assistance to respond,

1. give verbal cues and physical assistance.
Manipulate or guide the child through the entire skill. Hold on to the child's hands. Have child take a step forward or place the foot forward. Tell the child to bring the rear foot up to forward foot or to pick it up and move it near heel of lead foot; repeat sequence. Give the child specific verbal instructions throughout (in sign language, bliss symbols, action cues), such as "Put one foot forward," "Bring your other foot up," "Step-step together-step."

2. give verbal cues with demonstration.
Use a model or have the child watch you gallop forward. Then have the child perform the action. Use specific verbal instructions (as in 1 above with the modeling). You gallop five times on right foot then five times on left foot. Say to the child, "Step forward with same foot each time," "Lift your arms."

If a child can respond without assistance,

3. **give a verbal challenge in the form of a problem: "Who can . . . ?" "Show me how you can . . ."**
   a. Gallop on the footprints across the room (five right lead footprints, and then five left lead footprints.)
   b. Gallop to the chair, pick up the beanbag on the chair, and gallop back to me.
   c. Gallop around the hoops set up around the room.
   d. Gallop with a partner.
   e. Variation: Gallop to the beat of the drum.

4. **introduce self-initiated learning activities.** Set up the equipment and space for galloping. Provide time at the beginning of the lesson and free time for independent learning after the child understands the skills to be used. You may ask the child to create a game activity to play alone or with others (partner or small group) on or around the equipment.

5. **Variations:** Set up an obstacle course that includes galloping activities. Play a game, such as Cowboys and Indians, Gallop Tag, or Follow the Leader, that incorporates galloping activities.

GALLOPING: SKILL LEVEL 3

Performance Objective

The child with acquisition of Skill Level 2 or a level of performance appropriate for the child's level of functioning can maintain that level over six weeks.

Given activities that require the skill, the child can

1. play two or more games listed below at home or school, and
2. play with equipment selected by teacher and parent(s).

Skills to Review

1. Level 1 gallop. Step forward with lead foot followed by step with rear foot to heel of lead foot, and during
2. a brief period of nonsupport as rear foot approaches lead foot, shift weight forward, and then
3. gallop three or more times.
4. Level 2 gallop. With arms bent at sides, lift arms while transferring weight to forward foot and
5. lead with right or left foot, and then
6. gallop five or more times.

Action Words

Actions: Gallop, step

Objects: Arm, foot, lead foot, leg, rear foot

Concepts: Behind, do this, forward, front, look, ready, rear, show me, together, up

Games

- Cowboys and Indians
- Did You Ever See a Lassie/Laddie?
- Follow the Leader
- Freeze
- Gallop Tag
- Hill Dill
- Obstacle Course
- Train Station

TEACHING ACTIVITIES FOR MAINTENANCE

In Teaching

1. Provide the child with teaching cues (verbal and nonverbal, such as demonstration, modeling, imitating) for galloping that involve the skill components the child has achieved in compatible teaching and play activities. Bring to the child's attention the skill components he or she has already achieved. Provide positive reinforcement and feedback to the child.
2. Use games that require galloping and that involve imitating, modeling, and demonstrating.
3. Observe and assess each child's maintenance at the end of two weeks. Repeat at the end of four weeks (if maintained) and six weeks after initial date of attainment.

▲ Box in the skill level to be maintained on the child's Class Record of Progress. Note the date the child attained target level of performance (defined by teacher alone or co-planned with parents).

▲ Two weeks after attainment, observe the child. Is the level maintained? If child does not demonstrate the skill components at the desired level of performance, indicate the skill components that need reteaching or reinforcing in the comments sheet on the Class Record of Progress. Reschedule teaching time, and co-plan with parents the home activities necessary to reinforce child's achievement of the skill components and maintenance of attainment.

▲ Continue to observe the child, and reteach and reinforce until the child maintains that level of performance for six weeks.

▲ Plan teaching activities incorporating these components so that the child can continually use and reinforce them and can acquire new ones over the year.

▲ When the child can understand it, make a checklist poster illustrating the child's achievements. Bring the child's attention to these skill components in various compatible play and game activities throughout the year. Have the child help others—a partner or a small group.

In Co-Planning with Parent(s)

1. Encourage the parent(s) to reinforce the child's achievement of the skill components in everyday play and living activities in the home.

▲ Provide key action words for the parent(s) to emphasize.

▲ Give the parent(s) a list of play and games to use in playing with the child, thus reinforcing the skill components the child has achieved and needs support to maintain.

▲ Give the parent(s) a list of galloping activities that can be done at home with the child, such as
   a. Galloping around play equipment such as jungle gym, ladders, sandbox.
   b. Galloping up and down "hills": sandboxes, snowbanks.
   c. Galloping around the backyard.
   d. Galloping around local school track.
   e. Variation: Galloping to music.

2. Set up a time every two weeks to interact with the parent(s) and exchange feedback on the child's progress.

SLIDING: SKILL LEVEL 1

Performance Objective

The child with ability to walk can slide a distance of 30 feet three consecutive times, demonstrating the following skill components:

Within a clear space of 30 feet, the child can

1. step sideways with one foot followed by movement of trailing foot to position next to lead foot, and

2. transfer weight from following foot to lead foot, and then

3. perform three of these cycles on one foot.

Action Words

Actions: Move, slide, step

Objects: Arm, foot, lead foot, leg

Concepts: Around, lead, left, look, ready, right, show me, sideways

Games

- Circle Tag
- Did You Ever See a Lassie/Laddie?
- Drop the Flag
- Follow the Leader
- Giants and Dragons
- Hill Dill
- Indian Walk Through the Woods
- Obstacle Course
- Poison
- Round the Sun
- Simon Says
- Train Station

TEACHING ACTIVITIES

If a child requires assistance to respond,

1. give a verbal cue and physical assistance.
Manipulate or guide the child through the entire skill. Face the child and hold the child's hands. Slide with the child for several cycles (step together, step), then drop hands and continue. Give the child specific verbal instructions throughout (in sign language, bliss symbols, action cues), such as "Slide with me," "Step to the side, move your foot next to this one," "Do it again."

2. give a verbal cue with demonstration.
Use a model or have the child watch you slide, emphasizing the sideways step followed by moving the trailing foot to a position next to the lead foot in a continuous motion. Then have the child perform the action. Use specific verbal instructions (as in 1 above with the modeling).

If a child can respond without assistance,

3. give a verbal challenge in the form of a problem: "Who can . . . ?" "Show me how you can . . ."
a. Step sideways to this mark, then slide your other foot to this one.
b. Slide on all the taped marks. Slide across the room and touch the wall. Do it back to me.
c. Slide to the chair, slide around it, and come back to me.
d. Variations: Slide on the footprints on the floor. Slide to the beat of music.

4. introduce self-initiated learning activities.
Set up the equipment and space for sliding. Provide time at the beginning of the lesson and free time for independent learning after the child understands the skills to be used. You may ask the child to create a game activity to play alone or with others (partner or small group) on or around the equipment (carpet squares, taped lines).

5. Variations: Set up an obstacle course that includes colored tape, obstacles (slide, jump box, chair, or ladder) to slide around. Play a game, such as Circle Tag, Round the Sun, or Follow the Leader, that incorporates sliding activities.

SLIDING: SKILL LEVEL 2

Performance Objective

The child with acquisition of Skill Level 1 can slide three consecutive times, demonstrating the following skill components:

Within a clear space of 30 feet, the child can

4. with trunk maintained in upright posture and
5. body turned sideways to desired direction of travel,
6. step sideways for series of five cycles to right; repeat to the left.

Skills to Review

1. Step sideways with one foot followed by movement of trailing foot to a position next to lead foot, and
2. transfer weight from following foot to lead foot, and then
3. perform three of these cycles on one foot.

Action Words

Actions: Move, slide, step

Objects: Arm, foot, lead foot, leg

Concepts: Around, lead, left, look, ready, right, show me, sideways

Games

- Circle Tag
- Did You Ever See a Lassie/Laddie?
- Drop the Flag
- Follow the Leader
- Giants and Dragons
- Hill Dill
- Indian Walk Through the Woods
- Obstacle Course
- Poison
- Round the Sun
- Simon Says
- Train Station

TEACHING ACTIVITIES

If a child requires assistance to respond,

1. give verbal cues and physical assistance. Manipulate or guide the child through the entire skill. Stand facing the child. As the child slides, place a hand on each shoulder or side of waist and hold trunk upright. Have the child slide on taped marks on the floor, and emphasize weight transfer from following foot to lead foot. Give the child specific verbal instructions throughout (in sign language, bliss symbols, action cues), such as "Slide with me," "Step to the side, move your foot next to this one," "Do it again."

2. give verbal cues with demonstration. Use a model or have the child watch you slide, emphasizing the sideways step followed by moving the trailing foot to a position next to the lead foot in a continuous motion. Then have the child perform the action. Use specific verbal instructions (as in 1 above with the modeling).

If a child can respond without assistance,

3. give a verbal challenge in the form of a problem: "Who can . . . ?" "Show me how you can . . ."
a. Slide to the end of the three-foot inside line on the floor.

b. Slide around the marked circles on the floor.

c. Slide around the cones on the ground.

d. Slide to the chair with a beanbag on your head, and put it on the chair. Slide back.

e. Variations: Slide on the footprints on the ground; slide to the beat of music. Slide on various surfaces (cement, dirt, and grass).

4. introduce self-initiated learning activities.
Set up the equipment and space for sliding. Provide time at the beginning of the lesson and free time for independent learning after the child understands the skills to be used. You may ask the child to create a game activity to play alone or with others (partner or small group) on or around the equipment (carpet squares, taped lines).

5. Variations: Set up an obstacle course that includes colored tape, obstacles (slide, jump box, chair, or ladder) to slide around. Play a game, such as Circle Tag, Round the Sun, or Follow the Leader, that incorporates sliding activities.

SLIDING: SKILL LEVEL 3

Performance Objective

The child with acquisition of Skill Level 2 or a level of performance appropriate for the child's level of functioning can maintain that level over six weeks.

Given activities that require the skill, the child can

1. play two or more games listed below at home or school, and
2. play with equipment selected by teacher and parent(s).

Skills to Review

1. Level 1 slide. Step sideways with one foot followed by movement of trailing foot to a position next to lead foot, and then
2. transfer weight from following foot to lead foot, and
3. perform three of these cycles on one foot.
4. Level 2 slide. With trunk maintained in upright posture and
5. body turned sideways to desired direction of travel,
6. step sideways for series of five cycles to the right; repeat to the left.

Action Words

Actions: Mark, slide, step

Objects: Arm, foot, lead foot, leg

Concepts: Around, lead, left, look, ready, right, show me, sideways

Games

- Circle Tag
- Did You Ever See a Lassie/Laddie?
- Drop the Flag
- Follow the Leader
- Giants and Dragons
- Hill Dill
- Indian Walk Through the Woods
- Obstacle Course
- Poison
- Round the Sun
- Simon Says
- Train Station

TEACHING ACTIVITIES FOR MAINTENANCE

In Teaching

1. Provide the child with teaching cues (verbal and nonverbal, such as demonstration, modeling, imitating) for sliding that involve the skill components the child has achieved in compatible teaching and play activities. Bring to the child's attention the skill components he or she has already achieved. Provide positive reinforcement and feedback for the child.
2. Use games that require sliding and that involve imitating, modeling, and demonstrating.
3. Observe and assess each child's maintenance at the end of two weeks. Repeat at the end of four weeks (if maintained) and six weeks after initial date of attainment.

▲ Box in the skill level to be maintained on the child's Class Record of Progress. Note the date the child attained target level of performance (defined by teacher alone or co-planned with parents).

▲ Two weeks after attainment, observe the child. Is the level maintained? If child does not demonstrate the skill components at the desired level of performance, indicate the skill components that need reteaching or reinforcing in the comments sheet on the Class Record of Progress. Reschedule teaching time, and co-plan with parents the home activities necessary to reinforce child's achievement of the skill components and maintenance of attainment.

▲ Continue to observe the child, and reteach and reinforce until the child maintains that level of performance for six weeks.

▲ Plan teaching activities incorporating these components so that the child can continually use and reinforce them and can acquire new ones over the year.

▲ When the child can understand it, make a check-list poster illustrating the child's achievements. Bring the child's attention to these skill components in various compatible play and game activities throughout the year. Have the child help others—a partner or a small group.

In Co-Planning with Parent(s)

1. Encourage the parent(s) to reinforce the child's achievement of the skill components in everyday play and living activities in the home.

▲ Provide key action words for the parent(s) to emphasize.

▲ Give the parent(s) a list of play and games to use in playing with the child, thus reinforcing the skill components the child has achieved and needs support to maintain.

▲ Give the parent(s) a list of sliding activities that can be done at home with the child, such as
   a. Sliding around the basketball court at the park.
   b. Sliding up and down grassy hills.
   c. Sliding down the street.
   d. Sliding around the merry-go-round at the park.
   e. Variations: sliding on the footprints on ground; sliding to the beat of music; sliding on various surfaces (cement, dirt, and grass).

2. Set up a time every two weeks to interact with the parent(s) and exchange feedback on the child's progress.

SKIPPING: SKILL LEVEL 1

Performance Objective

The child with ability to walk can walk-skip a distance of 30 feet three consecutive times, demonstrating the following skill components:

Within a clear space of 30 feet, the child can

1. perform a step-hop pattern (step forward on one foot with hop on same foot as foot contacts floor following step) and
2. repeat step-hop pattern from one foot to the other three times.

Action Words

Actions: Hop, skip, step, swing

Objects: Arm, foot, leg, skipping foot

Concepts: Around, erect, forward, high, look, near, other, ready, show me

Games

- Catching Fish
- Drop the Flag
- Follow the Leader
- Obstacle Course
- Skip Around the Block
- Skipping Hill Dill
- Skipping Poison
- Skipping Relay
- Skipping Tag
- Train Station

TEACHING ACTIVITIES

If a child requires assistance to respond,

1. give verbal cues and physical assistance.
Manipulate or guide the child through the entire skill. Stand in front of the child and hold the child's hands. Have the child step on one foot, then hop on the same foot in place. Repeat on the other foot, standing in place. Lift the child up when hopping. Give the child specific verbal instructions throughout (in sign language, bliss symbols, action cues), such as "Skip to me," "Step and hop on this foot," "Now step and hop on the other foot," "Step-hop, step-hop."

2. give verbal cues with demonstration.
Use a model or have the child watch you skip across the room, using step-hop pattern. Then have the child perform the action. Use specific verbal instructions (as in 1 above with the modeling).

If a child can respond without assistance,

3. give a verbal challenge in the form of a problem: "Who can . . . ?" "Show me how you can . . ."
a. Skip on the footprints on the ground.
b. Skip in place with a partner.
c. Variation: Skip to the beat of the drum.

4. introduce self-initiated learning activities.
Set up the equipment and space for skipping. Provide time at the beginning of the lesson and free time for independent learning after the child understands the skills to be used. You may ask the child to create a game activity to play alone or with others (partner or small group) with the equipment.

5. Variations: Set up an obstacle course that includes equipment (ladders, benches, boxes) to skip around. Play a game, such as Follow the Leader, Skip Around the Block, or Skipping Hill Dill, that incorporates skipping activities.

SKIPPING: SKILL LEVEL 2

Performance Objective

The child with acquisition of Skill Level 1 can skip a distance of 30 feet five consecutive times, demonstrating the following skill components:

Within a clear space of 30 feet, the child can

3. with foot of nonsupport leg held near floor during hop of skipping foot and

4. arms held near sides, swinging in opposition to leg action,

5. maintain erect upright posture and perform

6. step-hop pattern five or more times.

Skills to Review

1. Perform step-hop pattern. Step forward on one foot with hop on same foot as foot contacts floor following step, then

2. Repeat step-hop pattern from one foot to the other three times.

Action Words

Actions: Hop, skip, step, swing

Objects: Arm, foot, leg, skipping foot

Concepts: Around, erect, forward, high, look, near, other, ready, show me

Games

- Catching Fish
- Drop the Flag
- Follow the Leader
- Obstacle Course
- Skip Around the Block
- Skipping Hill Dill
- Skipping Poison
- Skipping Relay
- Skipping Tag
- Train Station

TEACHING ACTIVITIES

If a child requires assistance to respond,

1. give verbal cues and physical assistance. Manipulate or guide the child through the entire skill. Stand in front of the child and hold the child's hands. Have the child step on one foot, then hop on the same foot in place. Repeat on the other foot, standing in place. Lift the child up when hopping. Give the child specific verbal instructions throughout (in sign language, bliss symbols, action cues), such as "Skip to me," "Step and hop on this foot," "Now step and hop on the other foot," "Step-hop, step-hop."

2. give verbal cues with demonstration. Use a model or have the child watch you skip across the room, using step-hop pattern. Then have the child perform the action. Use specific verbal instructions (as in 1 above with the modeling).

If a child can respond without assistance,

   3. **give a verbal challenge in the form of a problem: "Who can . . . ?" "Show me how you can . . ."**

   a. Skip on the footprints across the room.

   b. Skip to the chair, pick up the beanbag, and come back again.

   c. Skip around the room or basketball court.

   d. Variation: Skip to the beat of the drum.

4. introduce self-initiated learning activities.
Set up the equipment and space for skipping.
Provide time at the beginning of the lesson and free time for independent learning after the child understands the skills to be used. You may ask the child to create a game activity to play alone or with others (partner or small group) with the equipment.

5. Variations: Set up an obstacle course that includes equipment (ladders, benches, boxes) to skip around. Play a game, such as Follow the Leader, Skip Around the Block, or Skipping Hill Dill, that incorporates skipping activities.

SKIPPING: SKILL LEVEL 3

Performance Objective

The child with acquisition of Skill Level 2 or a level of performance appropriate for the child's level of functioning can maintain that level over six weeks.

Given activities that require the skill, the child can

1. play two or more games listed below at home or school, and
2. play with equipment selected by teacher and parent(s).

Skills to Review

1. Level 1 step-hop pattern. Step forward on one foot with hop on same foot as contacts floor following step, then
2. repeat step-hop pattern from one foot to the other three times.
3. Level 2 step-hop pattern. With foot of nonsupport leg held near floor during the hop of skipping foot and
4. arms held near sides, swinging in opposition to leg action,
5. maintain erect upright posture and
6. repeat step-hop pattern five or more times.

Action Words

Actions: Hop, skip, step, swing

Objects: Arm, foot, leg, skipping foot

Concepts: Around, erect, forward, high, look, near, other, ready, show me

Games

- Catch Fish
- Drop the Flag
- Follow the Leader
- Obstacle Course
- Skip Around the Block
- Skipping Hill Dill
- Skipping Poison
- Skipping Relay
- Skipping Tag
- Train Station

TEACHING ACTIVITIES FOR MAINTENANCE

In Teaching

1. Provide the child with teaching cues (verbal and nonverbal, such as demonstration, modeling, imitating) for skipping that involve the skill components the child has achieved in compatible teaching and play activities. Bring to the child's attention the skill components he or she has already achieved. Provide positive reinforcement and feedback for the child.
2. Use games that require skipping and that involve imitating, modeling, and demonstrating.
3. Observe and assess each child's maintenance at the end of two weeks. Repeat at the end of four weeks (if maintained) and six weeks after initial date of attainment.
▲ Box in the skill level to be maintained on the child's Class Record of Progress. Note the date the child attained target level of performance (defined by teacher alone or co-planned with parents).
▲ Two weeks after attainment, observe the child. Is the level maintained? If child does not demonstrate the skill components at the desired level of performance, indicate the skill components that need reteaching or reinforcing in the comments sheet on the Class Record of Progress. Reschedule teaching time, and co-plan with parents the home activities necessary to reinforce child's achievement of the skill components and maintenance of attainment.
▲ Continue to observe the child, and reteach and reinforce until the child maintains that level of performance for six weeks.
▲ Plan teaching activities incorporating these components so that the child can continually use and reinforce them and can acquire new ones over the year.

▲ When the child can understand it, make a check-list poster illustrating the child's achievements. Bring the child's attention to these skill components in various compatible play and game activities throughout the year. Have the child help others—a partner or a small group.

In Co-Planning with Parent(s)

1. Encourage the parent(s) to reinforce the child's achievement of the skill components in everyday play and living activities in the home.

▲ Provide key action words for the parent(s) to emphasize.

▲ Give the parent(s) a list of play and games to use in playing with the child, thus reinforcing the skill components the child has achieved and needs support to maintain.

▲ Give the parent(s) a list of skipping activities that can be done at home with the child, such as
   a. Skipping as fast as you can to the fence in your yard.
   b. Skipping along the figure 8 marked on the ground.
   c. Skipping around the cones in the zigzag pattern of the obstacle course.
   d. Skipping around the mailboxes (or trees) on your street.
   e. Skipping up and down the hills in the park.

2. Set up a time every two weeks to interact with the parent(s) and exchange feedback on the child's progress.

Checklists:
Individual and Class Records of Progress

A checklist is an objective score sheet for each locomotor skill taught in the program. By observing and assessing each child's level of performance, you can identify the activities that will assist the child in reaching the performance objective. Use the same checklist to monitor the child's progress during instruction. When the child's performance level changes, you can upgrade the learning tasks (skill components) to the child's new skill level.

To Begin

Decide on one or more locomotor activities to be taught in the program. Become familiar with the description of the performance objective for each activity selected. Review the scoring key on the checklist. Plan assessing activities for the selected skills. The number will depend on the class size, the needs of the children, and the help available to you. Set up testing stations similar to the learning stations. Some teachers use free-play time (after setting up equipment for the objective to be tested) to observe the children.

1. Begin assessing at Skill Level 2 for the particular objective. If the child cannot perform at Skill Level 2, assess for Skill Level 1. If the child demonstrates the skill components for Skill Level 2 (i.e., with modeling, verbal cues, or no cues), the child has achieved functional competence. At the next skill level, Skill Level 3, the child demonstrates maintenance retention of the skill over time.

2. For some children with special needs, you may need to assess their levels of functioning before planning teaching activities. As in step 1, observe and assess the amount and type of assistance (cues) the child needs in descending order (i.e., from verbal cues to total manipulation).

Code	Amount and Type of Assistance
SI	Child initiates demonstrating the skill in the teaching and playing of activities
C	Child demonstrates the skill when given verbal cues with or without demonstration
A	Child demonstrates the skill when given partial assistance or total manipulation throughout the execution of the skill

Record, using the code above, the child's initial assistance level and progress in the comments column of the Class Record of Progress. For some children, this may be the most significant initial progress noted (i.e., from assistance to verbal cues and demonstration).

To Assess

1. Be sure all children are working on objectives at other stations while you are assessing at one station.

2. Set up the testing station beforehand. Make sure enough equipment is available for the skill to be tested.

3. Use a relay to test running, skipping, hopping, sliding, or galloping. Be sure the starting and ending lines are clearly marked. Divide children into groups of three or four. Assess one group or team at a time. Have each child take a turn on the command "Go" (not when tagged). At the end of the trials, record the child's performance on the score sheet.

4. To test jumping and climbing, have two or three students at a testing station

ready to be tested. (The other children in the class should be working at the other learning stations.) Each child takes a turn. At the end of the trials, record the child's performance on the score sheet.

5. You may need to modify the assessing activity for children's special needs by using inclines, providing a wider base and lower rise for steps, taking a child through the pattern or modeling the activity, or using sign language or an interpreter. Other modifications are individual assessment or free play with the equipment. Use mats or movable walls to help cut down on distractions.

To Adapt the Checklists

You can note children's skill components adaptations (i.e., physical devices or other changes) in the comments column on the Class Record of Progress. Other changes can be written under recommendations for individual children or the class. Modifications made for a child can be noted on the Individual Record of Progress. The Class Record of Progress can be adapted for an individual child. Record the name of the child rather than the class, and in the name column, record assessment dates. This adaptation may be needed for children whose progress is erratic, because it provides a base line assessment to find out where to begin teaching and evaluating the child's progress.

The Individual Record of Progress for the end-of-the-year report can be attached to the child's IEP (Individual Education Program) report. The record can also serve as a cumulative record for each child. Such records are very useful for new teachers, substitute teachers, aides, and volunteers, as well as parents. The format of the Individual Record of Progress can also be adapted for a Unit Report. The names of all the objectives for a unit—for example, walk-run endurance, running, catching a ball, and rolling a ball—are written rather than the names of the children. Book 8 illustrates the adaptation of the Individual Record of Progress for use in the Home Activities Program and for a Unit Report.

The checklists may be reproduced as needed to implement the play and motor skills program.

CLASS RECORD OF PROGRESS REPORT

CLASS _____   DATE _____

AGE/GRADE _____   TEACHER _____

SCHOOL _____

OBJECTIVE: CLIMBING UP AND DOWN STAIRS

SCORING:	SKILL LEVEL 1		SKILL LEVEL 2		SKILL LEVEL 3	PRIMARY RESPONSES:
	Up	Down	Up	Down		N = Not Attending
	Three Consecutive Times					NR = No Response
ASSESSMENT: _____Date **X** = Achieved **O** = Not Achieved / = Partially Achieved REASSESSMENT: _____Date ⊗ = Achieved Ø = Not Achieved	Places each foot on each step before stepping on next step, holding handrail or other support for balance	Places each foot on each step before stepping on next step, holding handrail or other support for balance	Alternates feet on each step while holding handrail or other support and maintaining balance	Alternates feet on each step while holding handrail or other support and maintaining balance	Two or more play or game activities at home or school demonstrating skill components over six-week period	UR = Unrelated Response O = Other (Specify in comments)
NAME	1	2	3	4	5	COMMENTS
1.						
2.						
3.						
4.						
5.						
6.						
7.						
8.						
9.						
10.						

Recommendations: Specific changes or conditions in planning for instructions, performance, or diagnostic testing procedures or standards. Please describe what worked best.

_____

_____

_____

_____

_____

CLASS RECORD OF PROGRESS REPORT

CLASS _____ DATE _____

AGE/GRADE _____ TEACHER _____

SCHOOL _____

OBJECTIVE: RUNNING

SCORING:	SKILL LEVEL 1			SKILL LEVEL 2			SKILL LEVEL 3	PRIMARY RESPONSES:
	Three Consecutive Times							

SCORING:

ASSESSMENT:

_____Date

X = Achieved

O = Not Achieved

/ = Partially Achieved

REASSESSMENT:

_____Date

⊗ = Achieved

Ø = Not Achieved

PRIMARY RESPONSES:

N = Not Attending

NR = No Response

UR = Unrelated Response

O = Other (Specify in comments)

Skill Level 1 columns:
1. Three or more periods of nonsupport (both feet alternately off ground)
2. Arms in opposition to legs, elbows bent
3. Foot placed near or on a line

Skill Level 2 columns:
4. Five or more periods of nonsupport (both feet off ground)
5. Heel-toe placement (moderate speed), not flatfooted
6. Swing leg, bent at 90 degrees

Skill Level 3 column:
7. Two or more play or game activities at home or school demonstrating skill components over six-week period

NAME	1	2	3	4	5	6	7	COMMENTS
1.								
2.								
3.								
4.								
5.								
6.								
7.								
8.								
9.								
10.								

Recommendations: Specific changes or conditions in planning for instructions, performance, or diagnostic testing procedures or standards. Please describe what worked best.

_____

_____

_____

_____

_____

CLASS RECORD OF PROGRESS REPORT

CLASS _____ DATE _____

AGE/GRADE _____ TEACHER _____

SCHOOL _____

OBJECTIVE: JUMPING

NAME	Prepares to jump forward, knees bent, arms extended behind body	Takes off and lands on both feet	Swings arms forward with thrust of legs	Takes off at 45 degrees	Knees bent, trunk flexed to absorb shock	Brings arms downward on landing, maintaining balance	Two or more play or game activities at home or school demonstrating skill components over six-week period	COMMENTS
	1	2	3	4	5	6	7	
1.								
2.								
3.								
4.								
5.								
6.								
7.								
8.								
9.								
10.								

Columns 1–3: SKILL LEVEL 1 (Three Consecutive Times); Columns 4–6: SKILL LEVEL 2; Column 7: SKILL LEVEL 3.

Recommendations: Specific changes or conditions in planning for instructions, performance, or diagnostic testing procedures or standards. Please describe what worked best.

_____

_____

_____

_____

_____

Class Record of Progress Report

CLASS _____ DATE _____

AGE/GRADE _____ TEACHER _____

SCHOOL _____

OBJECTIVE: HOPPING

SCORING:	SKILL LEVEL 1			SKILL LEVEL 2			SKILL LEVEL 3	PRIMARY RESPONSES:
ASSESSMENT: _____Date **X** = Achieved **O** = Not Achieved / = Partially Achieved REASSESSMENT: _____Date ⊗ = Achieved Ø = Not Achieved	Three Consecutive Times							N = Not Attending NR = No Response UR = Unrelated Response O = Other (Specify in comments)
	Moves forward, pushing off on either foot, landing on same foot	Weight balanced over support foot, maintains balance	Hops three times on one foot and three times on other foot	Nonsupport leg bent, foot carried near midline of body, with nonsupport foot near floor (6 inches)	Arms bent at elbows in front of body, uses forward arm lift with hop, to increase force	Hops five times on one foot and five times on other foot	Two or more play or game activities at home or school demonstrating skill components over six-week period	
NAME	1	2	3	4	5	6	7	COMMENTS
1.								
2.								
3.								
4.								
5.								
6.								
7.								
8.								
9.								
10.								

Recommendations: Specific changes or conditions in planning for instructions, performance, or diagnostic testing procedures or standards. Please describe what worked best.

_____

_____

_____

_____

_____

_____

CLASS RECORD OF PROGRESS REPORT

CLASS _____   DATE _____

AGE/GRADE _____   TEACHER _____

SCHOOL _____

OBJECTIVE: GALLOPING

SCORING:	SKILL LEVEL 1			SKILL LEVEL 2			SKILL LEVEL 3	PRIMARY RESPONSES:
ASSESSMENT: _____Date **X** = Achieved **O** = Not Achieved **/** = Partially Achieved REASSESSMENT: _____Date ⊗ = Achieved ∅ = Not Achieved	Three Consecutive Times							N = Not Attending NR = No Response UR = Unrelated Response O = Other (Specify in comments)
	Steps forward with lead foot followed by step with rear foot to heel of lead foot	Brief period of nonsupport as rear foot approaches lead foot; weight is shifted forward	Gallops three or more times	Arms bent at side, lifts arms while transferring weight to forward foot	Able to lead with right foot or with left foot	Gallops five or more times	Two or more play or game activities at home or school demonstrating skill components over six-week period	
NAME	1	2	3	4	5	6	7	COMMENTS
1.								
2.								
3.								
4.								
5.								
6.								
7.								
8.								
9.								
10.								

Recommendations: Specific changes or conditions in planning for instructions, performance, or diagnostic testing procedures or standards. Please describe what worked best.

_____

_____

_____

_____

_____

CLASS RECORD OF PROGRESS REPORT

CLASS _____ DATE _____

AGE/GRADE _____ TEACHER _____

SCHOOL _____

OBJECTIVE: SLIDING

SCORING:	SKILL LEVEL 1			SKILL LEVEL 2			SKILL LEVEL 3	PRIMARY RESPONSES:
ASSESSMENT: _____Date **X** = Achieved **O** = Not Achieved / = Partially Achieved REASSESSMENT: _____Date ⊗ = Achieved Ø = Not Achieved	Three Consecutive Times							N = Not Attending NR = No Response UR = Unrelated Response O = Other (Specify in comments)
	Steps sideways with one foot followed by other foot to a position next to lead foot	Transfers weight from following foot to lead foot	Series of three cycles on one foot	Maintains trunk in upright posture	Turns body sideways to desired direction of travel	Series of five cycles to right; repeat to the left	Two or more play or game activities at home or school demonstrating skill components over six-week period	
NAME	1	2	3	4	5	6	7	COMMENTS
1.								
2.								
3.								
4.								
5.								
6.								
7.								
8.								
9.								
10.								

Recommendations: Specific changes or conditions in planning for instructions, performance, or diagnostic testing procedures or standards. Please describe what worked best.

_____

_____

_____

_____

_____

CLASS RECORD OF PROGRESS REPORT

CLASS _____   DATE _____

AGE/GRADE _____   TEACHER _____

SCHOOL _____

OBJECTIVE: SKIPPING

SCORING:	SKILL LEVEL 1			SKILL LEVEL 2			SKILL LEVEL 3	PRIMARY RESPONSES:
ASSESSMENT: _____Date **X** = Achieved **O** = Not Achieved **/** = Partially Achieved REASSESSMENT: _____Date **⊗** = Achieved **Ø** = Not Achieved	Three Consecutive Times							N = Not Attending NR = No Response UR = Unrelated Response O = Other (Specify in comments)
	Step-hop pattern: Steps forward on one foot with hop on the same foot as foot contacts floor following step	Repeats step-hop pattern from one foot to the other three times	Foot of nonsupport leg held near floor during hop of skipping foot	Arms held near sides, swinging in opposition to leg action	Maintains erect upright posture	Repeats step-hop pattern five or more times	Two or more play or game activities at home or school demonstrating skill components over six-week period	
NAME	1	2	3	4	5	6	7	COMMENTS
1.								
2.								
3.								
4.								
5.								
6.								
7.								
8.								
9.								
10.								

Recommendations: Specific changes or conditions in planning for instructions, performance, or diagnostic testing procedures or standards. Please describe what worked best.

_____

_____

_____

_____

_____

INDIVIDUAL RECORD OF PROGRESS

Area: Locomotor Skills

CHILD: _____

LEVEL: _____

YEAR: _____

TEACHER: _____

SCHOOL: _____

Marking Period	*Date*
Fall Conference (white)	from____to____
Winter Conference (yellow)	from____to____
Spring Conference (pink)	from____to____
End-of-Year (cumulative) Report (blue)	from____to____

Preprimary Play and Motor Skills Activity Program

The Individual Record of Progress lists all of the objectives in which your child receives instruction during the play and motor skills program. The information reported on your child's Individual Record of Progress shows your child's entry performance and progress for a marking period. The end-of-the-year report represents your child's Individual Education Program (IEP) for the objectives selected and taught during the year.

Each objective is broken into small, measurable steps or skill components. This assists the teacher to assess what your child already knew before teaching began and to determine which step to start teaching first. One of the following symbols is marked by each step or skill component of the objective:

X = The child already knew how to perform this step before teaching it began.

O = The child did not know how to perform this step before teaching it began or after instruction of it ended.

⊗ = The child did not know how to perform this step before teaching it began, but did learn how to do it during the instruction period.

This information should be helpful to you in planning home activities to strengthen your child's play and motor skills.

Comments

_____
_____
_____
_____
_____
_____
_____
_____

CLIMBING UP AND DOWN

Date: _____

Climbs 4–8 steps (5- to 8-inch rise).

_____ Places each foot on each step before stepping on each step, holding handrail or other support for balance while climbing up.

_____ Places each foot on each step before stepping on each step, holding handrail or other support for balance while climbing down.

_____ Alternates feet on each step, holding handrail or other support while climbing up.

_____ Alternates feet on each step, holding handrail or other support while climbing down.

_____ Demonstrates above skills in two or more play or game activities at home or school over a six-week period.

RUNNING

Date: _____

Within a clear space walk-runs a distance of 30 feet.

_____ Three or more periods of nonsupport (both feet alternately off ground).

_____ Arms move in opposition to legs, elbows bent.

_____ Foot placed near or on a line.

_____ Five or more periods of nonsupport (both feet off ground).

_____ Heel-toe placement (moderate speed), not flatfooted.

_____ Swing leg, bent at 90 degrees.

_____ Demonstrates above skills in two or more play or game activities at home or school over a six-week period.

JUMPING

Date: _____

Within a clear space of 10 feet, jumps forward over a line a distance of one quarter of full vertical height attained.

_____ Prepares to jump forward, knees bent, arms extended behind body.

_____ Takes off and lands on both feet.

_____ Swings arms forward with leg thrust.

_____ Takes off at 45 degrees.

_____ Knees bent, trunk flexed to absorb shock.

_____ Brings arms downward on landing, maintaining balance.

_____ Demonstrates above skills in two or more play or game activities at home or school over a six-week period.

HOPPING

Date: _____

Within a clear space of 10 feet, hops.

____ Moves forward, pushing off on either foot, landing on the same foot.

____ Weight balanced over support foot and maintains balance.

____ Hops three times on one foot, and three times on the other foot.

____ Nonsupport leg bent, foot carried near midline of body, with nonsupport foot near floor (6 inches).

____ Arms bent at elbows in front of body, uses forward arm lift with hop to increase force.

____ Hops five times on one foot and five times on other foot.

____ Demonstrates above skills in two or more play or game activities at home or school over a six-week period.

GALLOPING

Date: _____

Within a clear space of 30 feet, gallops.

____ Steps forward with lead foot followed by step with rear foot to heel of lead foot.

____ Brief period of nonsupport as rear foot approaches lead foot; weight is shifted forward.

____ Gallops three or more times.

____ Arms bent at sides, lifts arms while transferring weight to forward foot.

____ Able to lead with right foot and left foot.

____ Gallops five or more times.

____ Demonstrates above skill in two or more play or game activities at home or school over a six-week period.

SLIDING

Date: _____

Within a clear space of 30 feet, slides.

____ Steps sideways with one foot followed by movement of trailing foot to a position next to lead foot.

____ Transfers weight from following foot to lead foot.

____ Series of three cycles on one foot.

____ Maintains trunk in upright posture.

____ Turns body sideways to desired direction of travel.

____ Series of five cycles to the left; five cycles to the right.

____ Demonstrates above skills in two or more play or game activities at home or school over a six-week period.

SKIPPING

Date: _____

Within a clear space of 30 feet, skips.

____ Performs step-hop pattern: Steps forward on one foot with hop on the same foot as foot contacts floor following the step.

____ Repeats step-hop pattern from one foot to the other three or more times.

____ Foot of nonsupport leg near floor during hop of skipping foot.

____ Arms held near sides, swinging in opposition to leg action.

____ Maintains erect upright posture.

____ Repeats step-hop pattern five or more times.

____ Demonstrates above skills in two or more play or game activities at home or school over a six-week period.

Games

Game Selection

The following game sheets will help you select and plan game activities. They include the names of the games in alphabetical order, formation, directions, equipment, locomotor skills, and type of play activity. Consider the following points when selecting games:

1. Skills and objectives of your program
2. Interest of the child
3. Equipment and rules
4. Adaptability of physical difficulty level in order to match each child's ability
5. Activity for healthy growth and development
6. Social play skill development, such as taking turns, sharing equipment, playing with others, and following and leading

Games can foster creativity. Children enjoy making up, interpreting, and creating their own activities, whether playing alone, with a partner, or with a small group. The time you take to provide opportunities for each child to explore and create will be well spent. One further note. Children can easily create or adapt games matched to their mobility, even if limited by crutches, braces, or wheelchairs. Locomotor activities involve moving from here to there. These children easily comprehend how to get to "there" with their own expertise for movement.

Following are some suggestions for adapting the physical difficulty level of games and a sequential list of social play development.

Adapting Games

To Change	Use	Example
1. Boundaries	Larger or smaller space	Make bases 10 or 20 feet apart for Base Running game.
2. Equipment	Larger or smaller sizes, weights, or heights, or specially adapted equipment for some children (such as guiderails, inclines rather than stairs, brightly colored mats)	Climb 5 or 10 stairs on ladder or jungle gym in Follow the Leader game.
3. Rules	More or fewer rules	In Toss-Jump-Pick game, toss beanbag three times— or eight times.

To Change	Use	Example
4. Actions	More or fewer actions to be performed at one time; play in stationary positions, using various body parts	Move two or four body parts at one time in Did You Ever See a Lassie/Laddie game.
5. Time of play	Longer or shorter time; frequent rest periods	In Popcorn game, jump for one minute—or five minutes.

To adapt games to other special needs, you might also use buddies and spotters, sign language gestures, or place the child near leader.

Sequential Development of Social Play

Sequence	Description	Example of Play Activity
Individual Play	Child plays alone and independently with toys that are different from those used by other children within speaking distance.	Child plays in sandbox with shovel and pail. Other children play in sandbox with boats, cups, etc.
Parallel Play	Child plays independently beside, rather than with, other children.	Child plays with beanbags alongside other children who are also playing with beanbags. No interaction between children.
Associate Play	Child plays with other children. There is interaction between children, but there are no common goals.	Child plays and follows other children, with train or wagon.
Cooperative Play	Child plays within a group organized for playing formal games. Group is goal directed.	Children play Follow the Leader or Duck Duck Goose with one or two leaders.

GAME SHEET LESSON PLANS

GAMES	ORGANIZATION	DESCRIPTION/INSTRUCTIONS	EQUIPMENT	SKILLS	TYPE OF PLAY ACTIVITY
Animal Tracks	Line X X X X X	Place footprints on floor. Have children jump on "tracks" that animal has left in "snow."	Tape or footprints	Jump, hop	Individual, small group, large group
Base Running	Circle 	Children stand on bases. Children run around bases. At signal, all stop and stand on closest base.	Bases or carpet squares; drum or whistle	Run, jump, hop, skip, gallop	Relay; small group, large group
Bunny Hop	Scattered X X X X X X X	Have children squat with knees and hands on mat. Hop with knees and arms as rabbit would. Children can pick up block at end of path and walk back to place.	Mat or carpet squares for "path"; block	Hop	Individual, partner, small group, large group

Game Sheet Lesson Plans

Games	Organization	Description/Instructions	Equipment	Skills	Type of Play Activity
Catching Fish	Scattered	Divide room in half with rope and two chairs. Children all stand in half of room, the river. The other side is pond. Story: Farmer wants to get some fish to put in pond, and goes to river looking for best fish. Tells fish to move in various ways at signal. At second signal, children stop and freeze. Last one to freeze must crawl under rope into pond. Fish in pond move on signal. When last one or two get caught, the game is over.	Rope, drum, or whistle	Run, jump, hop, skip, gallop, slide	Tag game; small group, large group
Circle Tag	Circle	Organize children into circle, facing in. Say, "I'm going to tag someone on the back. Then I'm going to slide around the circle, and the person I tag is going to have to slide fast and try to tag me. If he (or she) tags me, I have to tag someone else. If I get back to his (or her) spot without being tagged, he (or she) is 'it'."	None	Slide, gallop, run, skip, jump, hop	Tag games; small group, large group
Climbing Hills, Paths	Scattered	On a nature hike, children climb up paths or hills, using rocks and trees as support. Children can climb large rocks or jump down with supervision.	None	Climb, jump	Individual, partner, small group, large group

Game Sheet Lesson Plans

Games	Organization	Description/Instructions	Equipment	Skills	Type of Play Activity
Climbing over Snowbanks	Scattered T X X X X X X	Children climb up and over large piles of snow, digging their feet into the snow to climb.	None	Climb	Individual, partner, small group, large group
Climbing Races	Lines X X X X X X X X X X X X X X X X X X X	Arrange three or more climbing obstacle courses. At starting signal, have first child of each line follow a designated climbing path over blocks and steps. The children in each line follow until all have had a turn.	Step stool, tape, blocks, ladder	Climb, run, gallop, jump, slide, hop, skip	Relay; small group, large group
Climbing, Ropes, Frames	Lines X X X X X X X X X X X X X X	Children climb up and down, climbing ropes and frames in gym.	Climbing rope; climbing frame	Climb	Individual, partner, small group

GAME SHEET LESSON PLANS

GAMES	ORGANIZATION	DESCRIPTION/INSTRUCTIONS	EQUIPMENT	SKILLS	TYPE OF PLAY ACTIVITY
Crossing the Lake	Circle	When music starts, all students walk around circle, jumping over lake. When music stops, any student caught in lake must drop out.	Tape or chalk or ropes; drum or record player	Jump	Small group, large group
Did You Ever See a Lassie/Laddie?	Line or semicircle	Leader starts song, performs the activity. Children mimic movements.	Bar, beam, ladder, mats, stairs, boxes, handrails, incline ramp	Run, climb, jump, gallop, hop, skip, slide	Small group, large group
Drop the Flag	Circle	Choose one child to walk around outside of circle and drop flag behind feet of another. Second child picks up flag and chases first back to vacant spot in circle.	Scarf or beanbag; rope or chalk line	Run, skip, gallop, hop, slide	Tag game; small group, large group

Game Sheet Lesson Plans

Games	Organization	Description/Instructions	Equipment	Skills	Type of Play Activity
Duck Duck Goose	Circle T x x x x x x x x x	Children form circle. Teacher appoints "it," who walks around circle tapping each student on head and saying "duck." When "it" says "goose," tapped child turns and chases "it" around circle. "It" tries to get to "goose's" place before being tagged by "goose." If tagged, "it" must sit inside circle.	Beanbag or hand-kerchief (to drop behind "goose" instead of tapping)	Run	Tag game; small group, large group
Fast and Slow	Scattered x x x x x x x x	Teacher says, "Listen to the drum. Take a slide step every time you hear a beat. Slide slower when I beat slower. Slide faster when I beat faster. When I blow the whistle, I'm going to point the way I want you to slide. Slide to the wall. Slide to me, etc." Can do it with a partner.	Drum, tambourine, records, whistle	Slide	Individual, partners, small group, large group
Fish Net	Circle and scatter x x x x x x x x x x x x x x	Divide group into two parts: fish and net. Form a net by holding hands in circle. On signal, fish run around. Have net move by running after fish and lifting up hands to surround fish. If children drop hands, net has hole and fish can escape. Make "pond" where caught fish must stay. Children, holding hands, place fish in pond.	None	Run	Tag game; partner, small group, large group

Game Sheet Lesson Plans

Games	Organization	Description/Instructions	Equipment	Skills	Type of Play Activity
Follow the Drum	Scatter	All children gallop to drumbeat. When drum stops, all stop and stand still. Tell children to make their feet go like the drumbeat: gallop.	Drum	Gallop, skip, hop, run, jump	Small group, large group
Follow the Leader	Line or circle	Leader performs action. Children respond by mimicking action.	Stairs, boxes, ladders, slide, bar, beam, handrails, incline ramp	Run, jump, hop, skip, gallop, slide	Partner, small group
Freeze	Line or circle	Children move in time to music. "Freeze" when music stops.	Stairs, boxes, bar, beam, handrails, incline ramp	Run, climb, jump, gallop, hop, skip, slide	Small group, large group

Game Sheet Lesson Plans

Games	Organization	Description/Instructions	Equipment	Skills	Type of Play Activity
Gallop Tag	Circle	Children stand in circle. One child starts game by galloping around the circle and taps another on shoulder. Second child tapped tries to catch first child before first gets to second child's spot. If unsuccessful, second child then becomes tagger.	None	Gallop, skip, jump, hop, run	Tag game; small group, large group
Giants and Dragons	Lines	Divide group into two lines 15–20 feet apart: giants in castle and dragons in cave. At signal, giants tiptoe toward dragons' cave, and dragons get ready to chase. When giants are very close, teacher signals "Dragons are coming," and giants run home. If tagged, they become dragons.	Rope	Run, skip, jump, gallop, slide	Tag game; small group, large group
Hill Dill		Children form two lines. Begin with one tagger. Tagger says, "Hill Dill come over the hill." Children run to opposite line to avoid being tagged. Child tagged helps tagger tag other children next time.	None	Run, jump, hop, skip, gallop, slide	Tag game; small group, large group

Game Sheet Lesson Plans

Games	Organization	Description/Instructions	Equipment	Skills	Type of Play Activity
Hoop, Hop, Jump	Line X X X X X	Children walk to first hoop, hop into hoop, jump out. Walk to second hoop, jump in and hop out, and so on, repeating this pattern.	Hula hoops or chalked circles in row	Jump, hop	Small group, large group
Hopping Relay	Scatter x x x cones	Divide children into two lines. Have children hop around cones in zigzag fashion. When first person is finished, touch hand of next line to start.	Traffic cones	Hop, jump	Relay; small group, large group
Hopscotch (modified)	x x x → hop / hop / jump / hop / jump	Have two to four children play at one hopscotch board. Teacher says, "Throw beanbag in one of the boxes. Hop in first box, hop again, now jump with both feet, hop and jump. You can't hop in box where beanbag is—you have to jump over it."	Chalk, tape, bean-bag	Hop, jump	Individual, partner, small group, large group

Game Sheet Lesson Plans

Games	Organization	Description/Instructions	Equipment	Skills	Type of Play Activity
Hot Rods	(diagram: rectangular track with arrows labeled "pit stop")	When teacher says "go," hot rods run (or hop or do any other locomotor skill) two times around gym on colored line. When done, they sit on pit stop.	Colored masking tape to make track	Run, jump, hop, skip, gallop, slide	Individual, small group
Indian Walk Through Woods	Circle (diagram of X's arranged in a circle)	Tell a story about Indians who move quietly in woods. Tell children, "We are all going for an Indian walk through woods. Follow me. Walk in silence." Leader does movements; other children imitate. Instruct all children to run back to starting position at signal "Everyone run home."	Tires or hoops; outdoor play equipment, or trees and bushes	Hop, jump, skip, gallop, run, slide	Individual, partners, small group, large group
Jet Pilots	(diagram: row of X X X X X with line and arrow labeled "teacher")	Teacher is starter. Says, "Jet pilots, take off." Children run to other line. First one to other side is new starter.	None	Run, jump, hop, skip, gallop, slide	Relay; small group, large group

Game Sheet Lesson Plans

Games	Organization	Description/Instructions	Equipment	Skills	Type of Play Activity
Jump In and Out of Tires	Line X X X X X	As part of obstacle course, encourage children to jump into and out of hoops or tires.	Tires or hoops or taped circles on floor	Jump	Individual, partner, small group, large group
Jump, Rabbit, Jump	Line T xxx ⊗⊗⊗	First child in line jumps into first hula hoop or tire, then into second, third. When child jumps out of last hoop, he or she runs back to end of line. When first child is halfway down the row, the second child begins.	Hula hoops or tires or carpet squares	Jump	Relay; small group
Jump the Shot	Circle + + + + T + + + +	Children stand around circumference of large circle. Teacher stands at center, swinging ball or beanbag on rope in a circle on floor. Children jump over it as it approaches them.	10-foot rope and ball or small weighted object (beanbag) at one end	Jump, hop	Large group

Game Sheet Lesson Plans

Games	Organization	Description/Instructions	Equipment	Skills	Type of Play Activity
Jumping Races	Line X X X X X ⟶	Each child steps into a pillow-case. Jumps to finish line. Can hold beanbag or balloon between knees.	Pillowcases, bean-bags, balloons	Jump, hop, run	Race; small group, large group
Jumping Rope	Line X X X X X	While two leaders hold end, children jump over rope, gradually increasing height until someone misses. Can wiggle or shake rope.	Rope at least 4–5 feet long	Jump	Two or more, small group
Jungle Gym Tag	Scattered T X X X X X X X	Children try to tag each other while climbing to the top of jungle gym. One is tagger first. Child who gets tagged becomes tagger.	Climbing apparatus (jungle gym)	Climb	Tag game; small group

Game Sheet Lesson Plans

Games	Organization	Description/Instructions	Equipment	Skills	Type of Play Activity
Obstacle Course	Line X X X X X T	First child begins course; when first child completes second station, second child starts.	Side, stairs, cones, mats, barrel, boards, chairs, bars	All locomotor skills	Individual, partner, small group, large group
On and Off the Blanket	Circle	Have children stand around blanket. On signal "Everyone jump," all jump onto blanket. At "Everyone hop off," all hop off. Vary comments—fast, slow, loud, soft.	Old blanket or large square drawn with chalk or indicated with rope	Hop, jump	Small group, large group
Partner Hop	Scatter in pairs	Pair children and have pairs scatter. Hold partner's hand, and on signal all begin hopping. Teacher says, "Ready, hop, help hopping with your partner. Hop as long as you can."	None	Hop, jump	Partner, small group, large group

GAME SHEET LESSON PLANS

GAMES	ORGANIZATION	DESCRIPTION/INSTRUCTIONS	EQUIPMENT	SKILLS	TYPE OF PLAY ACTIVITY
Poison	Scatter	Children all pretend to be poison. Tell them: "Don't touch anyone. Run in slow motion. On command, stop, stand very still. Then run fast, don't touch anyone. If you are touched, you become poison, too."	10-foot circle on floor made with masking tape	Run, jump, hop, skip, gallop, slide	Tag game; small group, large group
Pop Goes the Weasel	Circle	Children stand in circle. Sing song. "Pop" is signal to jump. "All around the cobbler's bench, the monkey chased the weasel. The monkey thought t'was all in fun. Pop goes the weasel! "A penny for a spool of thread. A penny for a needle. That's the way the money goes. Pop goes the weasel!"	None	Jump	Partner, small group, large group
Popcorn	Circle	Half the children sit around circle; they are "heat." Children inside circle are "popcorn." When "heat" rises, "popcorn" starts to pop by jumping slowly. As "popcorn" gets hot, jump higher, faster.	None	Jump	Small group, large group

GAME SHEET LESSON PLANS

GAMES	ORGANIZATION	DESCRIPTION/INSTRUCTIONS	EQUIPMENT	SKILLS	TYPE OF PLAY ACTIVITY
Rig-A-Jig-Jig	Circle × × × × × × × × × T	All children stand on rope circle and sing song. One child walks around circle. "As (child's name) was walking down the street, down the street, down the street, a friend of his he (hers she) chanced to meet. Hi-ho, hi-ho, hi-ho! Rig-a-jig-jig and away we go, away we go, away we go, away we go, and away we go. Hi-ho, hi-ho, hi-ho." The word *friend* is signal for child to pick a partner. The two run or jump around circle. First child goes back to second child's spot; then second child moves around circle.	Rope for circle	Run, skip, jump, gallop, hop	Tag game; small group, large group
Rolling Down the Tube	Line × × × × ×	Set carpet tubes on incline. Have child place golf ball in tube, then run to other end, catching ball in cup.	Carpet rolls, plastic containers, or boxes; plastic golf ball	Run	Individual, partner, small group, large group
Round the Sun	Partners in double lines × × × × × × ↑ ◀ × × × × × × ↑ ◀	Have pairs of children line up, face each other, and hold hands. Say, "_____ and _____ are going to slide to the cone together; then they will come back to start. Go when I say go. Slide as fast as you can." (This game can use any locomotor skill.)	Traffic cones	All locomotor skills	Tag game, partner, small group, large group

GAME SHEET LESSON PLANS

GAMES	ORGANIZATION	DESCRIPTION/INSTRUCTIONS	EQUIPMENT	SKILLS	TYPE OF PLAY ACTIVITY
Skip Around the Block	Line (line diagram with xxxx and arrows around a rectangle)	Children line up. Say, "Let's skip around the block. Step and hop like this."	Four traffic cones, taped area	Skip	Individual, partner, small group
Skipping Hill Dill	Lines X X X X X (tape) T (tape) safe area	Line up children along tape. Teacher says, "I am 'it.' When I say 'Hill Dill, come over the hill,' everyone skip and walk to the safe area. I will try to tag you. Skip fast. If you are tagged, you must help me tag others."	Taped area	Skip	Tag game; large group, small group
Skipping Poison	Circle (circle diagram with x's around it) (taped circle)	Children stand within a circle. Teacher says, "Pretend everyone else in the circle is poison. If they touch you, you are poison, too. Don't let anyone touch you. Let's skip now."	10-foot circle with tape	Skip, jump, run, hop, gallop, slide	Tag game; small group

GAME SHEET LESSON PLANS

GAMES	ORGANIZATION	DESCRIPTION/INSTRUCTIONS	EQUIPMENT	SKILLS	TYPE OF PLAY ACTIVITY
Skipping Relay	Lines	Have children line up in two lines. On signal, children skip around traffic cones and back to end of line. When all children have had their turns, the game is over.	Two traffic cones	Skip, jump, run, hop, gallop, slide	Small group
Stop and Go	Circle	Arrange chairs in circle. Have children jump around the circle, and when drum stops, have them search for chairs. Children who don't find chairs come to inner circle and keep time to drumbeat by clapping.	Chairs, drum	Jump	Small group, large group
Thousand-Legged Worm	Circle	Song (tune of "Polly Wolly Doodle"): "Oh, tell me,' said the thousand-legged worm, 'has anyone seen a leg of mine? If it can't be found, I'll have to hop around on the other 999. Hop around, hop around on the other 999. If it can't be found, I'll have to hop around on the other 999.'" Children can hold on to one another's shoulders.	Drum	Hop, jump, skip, gallop, run, slide	Small group, large group

Game Sheet Lesson Plans

Games	Organization	Description/Instructions	Equipment	Skills	Type of Play Activity
Toss-Jump-Pick	Line (diagram: rows of X's with arrows to circles, marked T)	Children stand on box or stairs or on floor and toss beanbag in front of them on ground. Then jump down stairs or box and over beanbag, and pick up beanbag.	Stairs, boxes, beanbag	Jump	Individual, small group, large group
Train Station	Line (diagram: X X X X)	Unwind the rope to form path around the room. Place chairs to make 4 or 5 stations. Teacher says, "When you hear the drum, the train begins to move. We will be a jumping train. We'll stop at station to get sandwich. Then we'll be a hopping train to next station, where we will buy something to drink. Move around all stations." Children can decide locomotion pattern.	Ropes for train tracks; chairs or books to mark stations; drum or whistle	Run, jump, hop, gallop, skip, slide	Small group
Upstairs, Downstairs	(diagram: X X X with "stairs" labels and arrows)	On teacher's command, children walk along taped floor pattern and step up and down stairs around room.	Four sets of stairs placed around room; incline ramp	Climb	Individual, small group, large group